Meaning of a Disability

Meaning of a Disability

The Lived Experience of Paralysis

Albert B. Robillard

Temple University Press
PHILADELPHIA

Temple University Press, Philadelphia 19122

Published 1999
Printed in the United States of America

∞ The paper used in this publication meets the requirements of the American National Standard for Information Sciences—Permanence of Paper for Printed Library Materials, ANSI Z39.48-1984

Library of Congress Cataloging-in-Publication Data

Robillard, Albert B., 1943–
Meaning of a disability : the lived experience of paralysis / Albert B. Robillard.
p. cm.
Includes bibliographical references and index.
ISBN 1-56639-675-1 (cloth : alk. paper). — ISBN 1-56639-676-X (pbk. : alk. paper)
1. Robillard, Albert B., 1943– —Health. 2. Amyotrophic lateral sclerosis—Patients—Biography. I. Title.
RC406.A24R59 1999
362.1'9983—dc21
[B] 98-36637

To Divina

Contents

Acknowledgments

There are many people to thank for getting this book together.

Among the first are my supportive wife, Divina, and the most significant intellectual influence in my life, Harold Garfinkel. I met my wife in March 1982 on the small island of Pohnpei, in Micronesia. She was a public health nurse consultant for the World Health Organization. She was training health aides, nurses, and other health workers in village-based primary care health services. I was teaching mental health counselors at the Pohnpei State Hospital. I then held an appointment in the University of Hawaii Department of Psychiatry.

I followed Divina to Manila, where she was teaching nursing in the College of Nursing at the University of the Philippines, Diliman. We married in August 1982 and moved to Honolulu in the fall. We started working together in Micronesia. We traveled extensively, throughout the Marshall Islands and the Federated States of Micronesia, to the Northern Marianas, Guam, and the Philippines, and to Washington, D.C., the source of our funding.

Divina joined the faculty of the Department of Nursing at Kapiolani Community College, a part of the University of Hawaii. She held this position until the winter of 1992. In 1992, I had been hospitalized for pneumonia. The bout of pneumonia was related to my current condition, motor neuron disease. After we determined it would cost more to hire a nurse to care for me than her teaching salary could provide, she resigned from the faculty and became my full-time care provider. Divina has kept me alive with her expert care, kept me working, and kept me fully involved in family affairs. I owe her every breath I draw.

Harold Garfinkel was my professor at UCLA. I received my doctorate there in 1974. Harold, as he is called by his students, has remained a mentor and inspiration since my graduate student days.

In the late 1960s, Garfinkel gave a name to the kind of study he had been developing since his own graduate work at Harvard in the late 1940s. He called it ethnomethodology, after ethnomusicology, ethnobotany, ethnopharmacology, and other fields of study examining how local cultures constitute specific areas of practical knowledge—for example, making medicines out of indigenous plants. Ethnomethodology, however, is more than a cultural study. It collects and describes practices used to produce recognizable social structures, by the members of those structures, as ongoing ordinary events. Ethnomethodology is indifferent to all claims of objective knowledge, preferring to analyze any statement, its referents, or any witnessable state of the world as ongoing social accomplishments.

My first academic appointment was in the Department of Pediatrics at Michigan State University in East Lansing. I studied the work-site-specific utterances and bodily behavior of pediatricians. I was joined in this work by Chris Pack, another of Garfinkel's students. We tried, with some success, to describe and reproduce the locally recognizable practical methods used by pediatricians, children, and parents to produce clinical encounters.

After six years of studying pediatric doctor-patient-parent interaction, I moved to the University of Hawaii. I first joined the Department of Psychiatry. In addition to teaching medical students in their psychiatric clerkship, and teaching residents about clinical interaction, I was involved in developing and implementing a training course for mental health counselors in the Republic of the Marshall Islands, the Federated States of Micronesia, the Republic of Balau, and the Commonwealth of the Northern Marianas. Training medical students and residents was by now routine, but training mental health counselors in Micronesia was something else. The faculty from the Department of Psychiatry did not know the languages of Yap, Pohnpei, Kosrae, Palau, Chuuk, Guam, and Saipan. Furthermore, we had only a superficial knowledge of the very different cultures of each island group.

While participating in the training programs I began a study of the concerted methods of the faculty, methods that permitted them to get funding and pursue a culturally blind program of limited consequence to the local population. This investigation led to a conference and book on Western mental health services for the Pacific Islands, including Hawaii.

After six years of work in Micronesia a number of things happened. They would change the direction of my work. First, I began to feel the effects of what was apparently my present disease. I could no longer easily take the long flights to Micronesia and back. My Pacific Island work was based on my ability to travel and collect materials. I had to decide on another kind of Pacific Island academic work or accept that this endeavor had come to its end. Second, I was not entirely happy with the direction the Pacific Island work had taken. I felt I had strayed from ethnomethodology. Third, as I suffered the atrophy of my muscles and came to inhabit a new, unfamiliar body, I began to describe my experience in ethnomethodological language. Fourth, my wife, Divina, urged me to write an ethnomethodology of my changing body.

Garfinkel had always talked to Divina as if she were a full-fledged ethnomethodologist. He had visited Hawaii, and we had traveled to UCLA. He thought, since she was a registered nurse and taught nursing, that she would be interested in and aware of the behavioral details that made nursing a recognizable event for nurses and other interested parties. Garfinkel had years of experience in teaching nurses. He was correct about what natural interest my wife could have in ethnomethodology. My speaking of my changed body, and Divina's appreciation of what ethnomethodology could hold for my illness, pushed me toward doing a detailed ethnomethodology of my condition.

I have a series of other people to thank:

Steven Berman is my personal physician. For thirteen years he has been my health advocate. He has never imposed an unstated, but nevertheless inferred, text that closed my horizon for living a productive life. I appreciate his nonjudgmental attitude as much as his clinical expertise in infectious diseases.

William B. Weil was my chairman in the Department of Pediatrics at Michigan State University. He has been my connection to medical care and research on the mainland. He taught me most of what I know about the U.S. health care system.

I have four colleagues at the University of Hawaii to thank for their support. The first is Kiyoshi Ikeda, chairman of the Department of Sociology. Kiyoshi was the one who hired me, and he has been a steadfast backer of my writing, grant getting, teaching, and other pursuits. The next is Eldon Wegner, also of the Department of Sociology. He has helped me teach seminars in medical sociology, has fostered an intellectual environment in which I could thrive, and has encouraged my activities at the University of Hawaii.

Jack Bilmes, of the Department of Anthropology, has

been a soulmate in things ethnomethodological. I regret that I did not start working with Jack sooner. His knowledge of ethnomethodology and conversation analysis is freely offered. He has been a good and nonjudgmental critic, and I really enjoy his company. Jack is the most intellectually giving person I know.

The last colleague I have to thank is Deane Neubauer of the Department of Political Science at the University of Hawaii. When I joined the College of Social Sciences there, Deane was the Dean of the College. We found an immediate intellectual affinity, perhaps growing out of his prior appointment at the University of California, Irvine, where he, too, pursued an interest in ethnomethodology. Deane has been my biggest supporter, teaching seminars with me, co-authoring books, papers, and grant proposals, writing curricula, and sharing talented students. He has also been instrumental in solving problems in my personal life, coming every day when I was in the hospital, either repairing my house himself or getting good people to work on it, and coming over at a minute's notice. If anyone has been my guardian angel, it is Deane.

Donald Topping, former director of the Social Science Research Institute at the University of Hawaii, was essential in getting me the release time in which to write the book. Don has backed me for years. He read numerous versions of the chapters and offered constructive criticism.

When Don Topping resigned from the directorship of the Institute, Michael Hamnett took over as acting director. Mike has been just as vigorous in his support of the book as was Don.

Dean Richard Dubanoski, of the College of Social Sciences at the University of Hawaii, has been an invaluable stay in my existence in the College. We met in front of a grocery store in Majuro, Marshall Islands. Since that time, Dick has been a man standing in the background, encouraging me to keep working.

David Goode, a friend since graduate school at UCLA, was the first one to suggest that I write a book about my experience as a paralytic. He now teaches at the City University of New York, Staten Island. David made the initial contact with Temple University Press, which had published his groundbreaking study of blind-deaf girls, *A World without Words.* I am very thankful to David, who shares my origins in Queens, New York, for conceiving of the book and for his unfailing encouragement during its writing.

I put the entire manuscript into words by lip-signing to my student research assistants. I could not have written this book without their good-humored and critical assistance. Those who helped me are Genitte Alipio, Qian Miao, Loan Nguyen, Scott Okamoto, and SueLyn Tran. Haynes Leung, now graduated, typed the book proposal. I have to thank Andrea Leung, now a medical social worker and law student, who assisted me when I was in the hospital and who took many of the ethnographic notes I lip-signed to her. Yi-Ding Chen, Zhou Miao (now Leung), and Anthony Bichel worked on two of the chapters in this book.

Charon Pierson, a member of the School of Nursing faculty at the University of Hawaii, read and commented on four chapters. Charon is my graduate student. She is a far better ethnomethodologist than I.

The entire manuscript was copy-edited by my daughter, Adrienne Robillard. Adrienne is a recent graduate of the University of California, Santa Barbara. Having majored in English, she now works as a copy editor in San Francisco. What readability this book has is due to the efforts of Adrienne.

Frank Austin is the free-lance copy editor who straightened out my sentences and meticulously checked the references. I owe Frank a lot for improving my prose.

I thank my son, Thomas Robillard, for turning pages at home. He turns eight of ten pages. Even when he complains, he does so with such good humor that it is a joy to experience.

Many friends and colleagues encouraged me to write an ethnomethodology of my illness. Peter Manning, a sociologist at Michigan State, was first in line. Arthur Kohrman, a pediatrician at Northwestern, always knew the promise of ethnomethodology. John O'Neill of York University in Toronto has been a consistent personal and intellectual supporter. He read and commented on two chapters and the book proposal. Mike Featherstone, of the University of Nottingham, Trent, published and discussed my paper on anger in *Body & Society.* Mike really encouraged me to pursue ethnomethodological studies of illness. Rosanna Hertz, editor of *Qualitative Sociology,* provided needed guidance and encouragement.

Finally, I want to thank SueLyn Tran, one of my research assistants, for unconsciously changing the capacities of my other research assistants from lip-readers to caregivers. SueLyn learned to suction and feed me and took over most of my care in the office. The other assistants soon followed her role modeling. She soon mastered every aspect of my care. SueLyn quickly became and remains a close and trusted friend, as well as an advisor on all manner of topics. She gave me the glorious sense of independence, where I feel I can operate on my own. I cannot thank SueLyn enough.

I am grateful to Humanities Press for giving permission to republish "Communication Problems in the Intensive Care Unit." It appeared in *Qualitative Sociology* 17(1994): 383–95. I thank Sage Publications for permission to republish "Anger in-the-Social-Order." It was printed in *Body & Society,* 2 (1996): 17–30. Chapters 3 and 4 are based on these articles.

1 Telling the Story

It is hard to know how to begin. I have told the story of my illness many times, each telling designed for the conversationally revealed interests of the recipients. I have told the clinical history to physicians—neurologists, immunologists, and internists—but each telling at once searches for things not told before, looks for new angles, and responds specifically to each clinician's inquiry. I have told the story to a Hawaiian *kahuna,* a native healer. Her questions about where I had been in the Pacific Islands and what I had done on each island made me wonder whether my illness was a spiritual retribution for some misdeed on a small Micronesian atoll. (I had spent a summer on Ulithi Atoll in the Caroline Islands.) Her questions about my activities in Micronesia were echoed by my mother-in-law, who thought my first wife had put a curse on me. The *kahuna* also asked me about my activities in the Philippines, where I had traveled widely. I reviewed my life there and even sent a rice god back to the Mountain Province shop where I had purchased it. The statue was cracked and I thought it represented some kind of disequilibrium. It was this state of disorganization in my body and life that had brought on the debilitation of motor neuron disease. Motor neuron disease is also known as Lou Gehrig's disease, or ALS, amyotrophic lateral sclerosis.

I have told the story of my illness to countless acquaintances, friends, colleagues, relatives, and students. Each telling is a little different, designed to fit the perceived expectations of the recipients and to fit the evolving conversation. My wife, Divina, has heard most of the story's permutations and has collaborated, without having to be told, in fashioning the story to the spot in the conversation and to the listener—priest, neurologist, family internist, fundamentalist Christians who say they are praying for me, *kahuna,* new friends and old friends, neighbors, parents of my children's classmates, each relative according to our history with them, and many more types of people than I have space to name.

I will try to tell the most inclusive version of the history of my illness here, without being boring. But the reader will have to remember that inclusiveness is a recipient-designed phenomenon. Because I do not know my readers, there may be some whose interests I will miss.

It is hard to know when the illness began. Carleton Gajdusek, a 1976 Nobel laureate in medicine, brought to our house by a mutual friend, said that the neuromuscular disease may have been developing for decades. I had told Carleton that I had fasciculation, or twitching, in the legs while in graduate school at UCLA in the 1970s and had them looked at by the school's neurology department. I was told they were benign fasciculations.

When Gajdusek said that the disease could have been, and must have been, developing over a long time, this made me rethink every symptom. Although I hate to admit that I gave a Nobel Prize–winner more creditability than the *kahuna,* I did the same retrospective life evaluation at Gajdusek's behest. But instead of remembering every Pacific island and atoll I had been on, examining my time there for any social offense, for Gajdusek I examined my memory for the onset of every twitch and muscle weakness. This examination went on long after he had left the house, becoming a constant theme of reflection, reinforcing every ontological doubt about the integrity of my body. I asked myself if my body had been undergoing the motor neurological breakdown all along. Had I been inhabiting a diseased, pathological body all these years? It certainly changed my history, at least when I had occasion to reflect upon it.

My responses to Gajdusek's interrogations and declarations—as well as the conversations with the *kahuna,* my mother-in-law, friends, and clinicians—set off an intense retrospective examination of my life. The search was either for the onset of symptoms or for the suspected cause of my condition. The intensity of these interrogations and my participation in them increased, at least for a while, as I became visibly more disabled and lost muscle mass. After I had become disabled and most friends and colleagues had witnessed my condition for a while, it became old news, at least to my face.

Onset

After my appointment at UCLA with the Department of Neurology in the 1970s to check out muscular twitching in the legs, I thought nothing about a possible neuromuscular disease until the mid-1980s. I started having twitching and cramps in the right upper arm and shoulder. I noticed a loss of strength in my right arm, as well as a hypersensitivity to touch in that arm. I once had trouble holding my briefcase in New York's JFK Airport while on a business trip to Washington, D.C., to look for additional grant money. The trip combined business with pleasure: a short excursion to my home town of Great Neck, Long Island. I merely thought I was tired from a hectic week. My hand muscles cramped up and I had to shift my briefcase to my left hand constantly as I walked around the airport looking for a flight to Chicago with a connection to Honolulu.

The fasciculations continued in my right arm and shoulder for about six months. At first I had no atrophy of the muscles there. I tried rest, reducing stress, joining a gym, and eating nutritious food. Yet even though I gained strength in the other parts of my body, I continued to experience cramping and gradual loss of strength in my right arm.

I joined the same health club as my brother, and recruited my brother-in-law as well. I started going to the gym three or four times a week. I really enjoyed lifting weights and soaking in the hot Jacuzzi after workouts. I would always go with either my brother or brother-in-law, and often both would accompany me. However, I found it increasingly difficult to do overhead presses. Soon, I had trouble doing bench presses. I would often skip these parts of the workout, even though this would provoke negative comments from my brother.

I would often go to my sister's house after a strenuous session at the health club. I found myself tired, in need of a breather, and I wanted to visit with her and my brother-in-law before driving back to my apartment in Honolulu. Sometimes, after a heavy workout, I would sit down in her house and feel my muscles shake. I would call this to her attention and she would observe the shaking in tiny bundles of muscles in my arms and legs. She encouraged me to see a physician, as did my wife.

I had a friend who was an internist. I had worked with him when I was in the Department of Psychiatry in the medical school at the University of Hawaii. I did not then have a personal physician in the state, having come to the University of Hawaii from Michigan State University's College of

Human Medicine. Until 1985, nothing had happened to me that would prompt me to go to the doctor.

I made and kept an appointment with my friend the internist. He asked me about my life since I had left Michigan for Hawaii. He knew I had been traveling extensively in Micronesia for the College of Medicine for three years. He asked if I were still involved in training mental health workers in Micronesia. I told him I had written several successful grant applications to the National Institute of Mental Health since joining the sociology department. I was still traveling to the islands of Micronesia every three months. These trips would take me out of town and the country for half the year.

The internist had also been involved in Micronesian work for the medical school and knew the "classic" underdeveloped conditions of the islands, as well as the long distances between them. He also knew that I had undergone a lot of stress related to a marital breakup in the early 1980s and an immediate remarriage. Furthermore, we shared a general dissatisfaction with the administration of federal grants at the medical school. His first diagnosis was that I was suffering from stress and overwork. He recommended that I relax by taking off early from work each day and going for a walk with my wife in Ala Moana Beach Park. I did this, thoroughly enjoying the sunsets across the Pacific.

I continued the regimen of working out at the health club, and I especially enjoyed the newly added time with my wife in the park. We would walk, looking at and discussing people. Divina made a conscious effort to talk my numerous anxieties away. As we ambled along she would tell me to relax and make me laugh at the people we saw.

Despite the workouts and walks, I slowly grew weaker. I also began to notice some shrinkage in the muscle mass in my right shoulder girdle and in my right arm. The fingers of that hand would independently move, which became a source of embarrassment. To keep them out of sight and away from comment, I would hold my hands behind my back. I thought I looked like Prince Philip.

My handwriting began to deteriorate. The muscles in my right hand would suddenly cramp in midsentence. Most often my fingers would extend in a rigid position, requiring some form of massage with my left hand to relax them. This condition affected only my right hand. My left arm and hand remained normal.

The loss of handwriting ability revealed a host of new problems. First, my job as a research professor required signing purchase orders for equipment and supplies, student-workers' time sheets, audits of grants and contracts, and forms when I hired new research assistants. In my other role as a teaching professor, I was even more locked in to writing by hand. I increasingly found I could not make intelligible corrections and comments on student papers. I began to use my computer to write my criticisms, clipping the printouts to the front of each paper. I still could type.

I had students sign my name to forms. This caused some immediate difficulties. I would never have thought a university had signature inspectors. I was wrong. Purchase orders were returned, with notes saying the signature did not match my previous signatures. Fiscal officers came out of the walls, telling me I couldn't do this. I was directed to get a power of attorney for the person signing the forms on my behalf. I considered doing so for one of my student assistants, but immediately realized that, as close as I was to them, they were transitory and soon graduated. My situation would require a regular and expensive renewal of power of attorney. Several colleagues, hearing of my predicament, volunteered to fill the role. I resisted this kind offer; the flow of paperwork was so intense that I would have to be chasing them around daily, and it was hard enough to get in touch with them in the best of circumstances.

The problem was solved when my wife got a power of attorney for me. She made arrangements with multiple offices on campus to witness that they would know she would be lawfully signing my documents. This took a lot of legwork, and some people still rejected the signature. To clear up this trouble, we deposited notarized copies of the power of attorney with each overview executive, such as the office of the dean and the office of research administration.

Years later, when my disability had spread my fame to almost every corner of the campus, especially after a feature story on the front page of the *Honolulu Star-Bulletin,* the need for a consistent signature and a power of attorney evaporated. I could have any of my student research assistants sign for me. The many divergent signatures—on student-workers' time sheets, purchase orders, grade sheets, change of grade records, and the many graduate student forms—were not questioned.

Philippines

About the time the muscles in my right hand were falling apart, I was named a Fulbright Research Professor. I had applied for this special nonteaching award to be used in the Association of Southeast Asian Nations (then comprising Philippines, Thailand, Indonesia, Singapore, Malaysia, and Brunei) almost a year before. I had planned seven months of research in the Philippines on the organization of community-based health services. Divina had been a faculty member in an innovative training institute in that country for community-based health care workers. She was my introduction, years before, to the worldwide movement toward low-cost, community-based health care. I visited my wife's former place of employment, the University of the Philippines Institute of Health Sciences in Tacloban, Leyte, both before and after we were married. I met many of her colleagues in community health at Tacloban, at the Western Pacific Office of the World Health Organization in Manila, and at the main campus of the University of the Philippines in Diliman.

Even though we suspected something was wrong with my health, we made preparations to go to Manila for seven or eight months. I decided I wanted to do research at Ateneo de Manila University, a Jesuit school. The priest of the University of Hawaii Newman Center, a Roman Catholic church I attended, was a former professor of sociology at Ateneo, and he wrote a letter of sponsorship for me. With his help, I became a research associate with the Institute of Philippine Culture (IPC) at the Ateneo de Manila University in Quezon City.

We made furious last-minute preparations to pack our entire apartment and put the contents into storage. We were living in a one bedroom apartment on the twenty-second floor, and Divina and I had decided that when we returned from Manila we would move into a house. We had run out of room for our frequent visitors and for my two children from my first marriage. During the mad-dash packing, the muscles in my right arm frequently cramped. Once, my right bicep flexed and then cramped and I could not get it to relax for about half an hour. The episode left signs of torn and bleeding muscles below the skin.

Our first task, once we had reported in at the university, was to find a rental house. The search was exhausting. I could not decide whether the fatigue stemmed from my apparent illness or from the difficulty of moving around metro Manila in bumper-to-bumper traffic and awful air pollution. But, whatever the cause, my wife and I spent a lot of time sleeping in the hotel operated by the University of the Philippines School of Travel Management. While we were feeling discouraged about finding an appropriate rental, one that would accommodate our many expected visitors, we received a call from a friend who told us that she was willing to vacate her house and rent it to us. Having visited there, we knew the five-bedroom, Spanish-style house built around an inner courtyard would be more than suitable. We moved in the next week.

With a furnished house to call home, Divina and I next searched for a car and for maids to occupy the house while we traveled around the Philippines. We acquired a three-year-old Ford sedan from a Chinese fellow living in Caloocan, the town immediately north of Manila. It had a manual transmission. After six months, my right hand had become so weak that shifting was a problem. In heavy traffic, the norm in Manila, my hand would slip off the knob of the floor-mounted gear lever and the car would come to a halt, provoking much honking. My wife suggested we hire a driver. We did.

My mother-in-law arranged for us to hire two maids. We already knew them and felt comfortable with them. They cleaned the big house and cooked the meals, permitting us a life of luxury. The maids were in the house twenty-four hours a day, taking one day off a week. We bought a queen size bed and a Sony television. We were all ready to live in Manila.

I set up an office in the one air-conditioned room of the house. I installed my portable computer and arranged boxes around the floor to hold the materials I expected to collect. Through a friend of my wife, Jimmy Tan, we made appointments at various church-related and secular nongovernmental health organizations. I visited AKAP, a church-related organization that sets up community-based primary care health delivery systems, and an agency concerned with the health of workers in the booming semiconductor industry. Most of the employees were girls and young women from the provinces, who were being put at risk by routine exposure to acids and other toxic substances. I met with members of the National Council of Churches, a Protestant group, which had many community-based primary care organizations in the northern parts of Luzon. I also visited a Catholic group that ran community-based primary care delivery systems in the Visayas and in Mindanao. I frequently heard that the organizations running community-based primary care programs were considered subversive by the Philippine government. I was told it was dangerous to be around persons involved in them and that President Ferdinand Marcos's goons were on patrol for what they considered the leftists running primary care. One time, I was warned that even to be seen visiting an order of nuns that ran community-based primary care services would get me arrested.

I got a bit frustrated about making contact with a Manila-based community health service program. Many of those involved were suspicious that I might be a CIA agent. Of course, these charges must be understood as arising in the hysteria of the last days of the Marcos administration. Men and women were disappearing. Bodies were being found every day. I could see I was not making progress in the Manila programs, and, on Divina's advice, I decided to go south and see if I could find other organizations to study.

Again with the help of Jimmy Tan, I made contact with a church-based primary care program in Tacloban, on the island of Leyte in the central Philippines. We flew south and met with a nun who administered community development programs on Leyte. She recommended that my wife and I visit two primary care programs, one urban and one rural. First, we went to a clinic in a church building in the middle of Tacloban; after it closed for the day, we visited the neighborhood where the patients lived. One week later, we went to see the other program, about sixty miles southwest of Tacloban. It was in the most rural place I have ever been to, with no electricity and no piped water. Yet the thatched huts, made from the nipa palm, were picturesque. It was the most impressive self-supporting community health program I have seen. The villagers backed it with common agricultural goods, mostly rice, which they marketed in Tacloban.

During the flight down to Tacloban and while walking around the town, I suffered many muscle cramps. I did a tremendous amount of walking in the city and in the rural village. I often felt exhausted at night, and went to sleep hoping that the next day I would awake refreshed. However, sunrise brought no refreshment, and the hot and humid weather drained me. I had stayed in Tacloban before and had not been so fatigued. The way my body felt worried me.

Divina and I returned to Manila with lots of material. I was happy we were making progress. I spent two weeks writing up my notes on the computer. After visiting more Manila-based community health organizations, we started to plan a trip to Davao in Mindanao. After a one-hour flight south, we caught the shuttle bus to the Davao Insular Hotel. On the road we had to stop while the Philippine Army cleared a field of Muslim separatist rebels. The driver of the minibus turned off the engine, and I could hear a strange quiet descend on the line of cars, buses, and trucks. My apprehensiveness soared as I waited for the sound of gunfire. The muscles in my arms began to twitch and my shoulders began to shake.

The danger passed, and we arrived at the hotel. It was a beautiful place, next to Davao Bay. We went swimming in the large hotel pool. After we returned to the room, we called Jimmy Tan, who had come down from Manila about two days before us. Jimmy had been the medical director of the Mindanao Catholic Health Services Program, a community-based primary care organization. It was supported by overseas donors, mainly British Catholics. We wanted to observe two of its programs.

The first of these was outside Davao, about a fifty-minute drive to the west, in a rural barrio. The place had been torn apart by the guerrilla war raging around Davao. There were burnt-out cars and trucks everywhere. I had a hard time concentrating on the health program. My eyes kept going back to the burned homes and vehicles. While we were in the village, a company of Philippine marines patrolled nearby, looking for members of the New People's Army, the Communist insurgency.

Divina and I learned how the barrio program was organized and what services it offered. We met with the local principals in the program and then with the village leaders, mainly the *barangay* captain. We toured the village and observed many public health problems. There was, for example, no running water; the villagers had to walk some distance to an open well, shared by three barrios. Another public health problem was head injuries caused by falling coconuts. The village was next to an operating copra plantation.

The next day we went to Agdao, a slum district of Davao. Much of Agdao, typified by one-room shacks supported by stilts, is built over Davao Bay. I did something there that would lead me to seek immediate medical attention in Manila. I always prided myself on my sense of physical balance. I think I developed it to an extraordinary degree when I was a boy, standing on deck in big ground swells off the southern coast of Long Island, where my family boated and fished from April to late November.

I tried to walk on the narrow boards that connected the houses in Agdao. I started out from the shore, trying to reach the first of the stilt houses. I began to have a hard time, sweating and trembling. I got only six feet from shore when I fell into the water. Luckily, it was low tide and I landed in shallow water and the underlying mud. It was not so much the falling as it was the trembling and shaking from muscle exhaustion that bothered me. I decided then that we would go to one of my wife's former colleagues, a physician, and ask for an appropriate referral in Manila.

When we eventually returned to our house, we went to see Ed Gonzales and asked him to think about my symptoms and make a referral. He put us in touch with a neurologist in the Manila Medical Center. The neurologist, a woman trained in the United States, told us she suspected I had amyotrophic lateral sclerosis. She did not know for certain and asked to schedule an electromyogram, a test of the electrical conduction of the muscles, at Philippine General Hospital. Then, she added that this was a life-threatening disease and that if I could go to the States for diagnosis and treatment it would be better.

UCLA

When Divina and I returned to our rental house in Teachers' Village, near the University of the Philippines, I jumped on the phone and called Harold Garfinkel. Garfinkel had chaired my dissertation committee at UCLA. He held a joint appointment in the Department of Psychiatry, housed in the Neuropsychiatric Institute (NPI) in the medical center. I told him what had been happening with my health and asked him to set up a neurological workup at the NPI. He said he would get in touch with Ed Shneidman and ask him to schedule the examination. Garfinkel said he would call back the next afternoon and tell me what had developed.

When I next spoke with Garfinkel, he related that everything had been set up for the next Monday. I then had to arrange for my wife and me to return to Los Angeles. It was summer and every plane was booked. In a feverish attempt to get to Los Angeles, we bought a ticket for Taipei, with a connecting flight to Los Angeles. The next day, China Airlines called us and said the connecting flight had been canceled. We went back to the travel agent to get our money back and to complain. The travel agent came up with an alternative: fly to Hong Kong and wait for eight hours for a Singapore Airlines flight to Los Angeles. The price was a little bit more. We accepted the alternative.

Numbed by having recently been told of a fatal disease, we flew west for two hours on Cathay Pacific Airlines to Hong Kong. Our attention was diverted outward as we made the tricky descent between buildings and approached the city's old airport. Once we got off the plane, we entered the long hall that makes up all of Kai Tak Airport. We would sit and walk about for eight hours while we waited for our flight. The Hong Kong airport is an interesting place to watch people. When the Singapore 747 rolled up and the Los Angeles flight was announced, we felt like we had been saved from an eternity of waiting.

The flight was enjoyable, and we came to understand why Singapore is rated the best international airline; the service cannot be compared to anything provided by U.S. carriers. I will always remember our cabin attendant, a man from India. After fifteen hours, we landed in Los Angeles and were picked up by my wife's uncle. We drove to a section two miles north of downtown, by Vermont Avenue. We were very tired and went to sleep right away. The next day was Monday, the day of my appointment at UCLA.

By arrangement, we met Garfinkel in his office. We then walked south, across the campus, to the medical center. We arrived at Shneidman's office at the NPI. He treated me like a returning student of his own, expressing great interest in what I was doing in the Philippines and in Micronesia. Between his questions about my studies, he asked many other questions about my condition. After about an hour of conversation, Shneidman got on the phone to the director of the NPI. He related my health complaints, who I was, and that I had just flown in from Manila; he then asked the director who I could see. An appointment was set for the next day.

We drove to UCLA from my wife's uncle's house on Tuesday. We met a friendly, balding, sandy-haired neurologist in his green-tiled laboratory. He took an extensive history and was very interested that I had undergone a neurological workup when I was a graduate student at UCLA. He asked me repeatedly the name of the neurologist I had consulted. I could only describe the appearance of the man. I told this second neurologist that the diagnosis from my earlier exam was benign fasciculations. He told me he would get the microfilm record of my past visit.

After taking the history, the neurologist asked me to sit on a bed. He explained he wanted to examine me and then give me an electromyogram. Afterward, he asked us to sit and talk. He said the clinical picture was unclear and he could not tell what was wrong with me. We asked him if I had a fatal neurological condition. He assured me I was not going to die. He asked me to have a magnetic resonance imaging (MRI) test. He explained that the MRI unit at UCLA was fully booked and that I would have to go to the Huntington Medical Foundation in Pasadena on Wednesday, the next day. I agreed.

Our appointment was for 7 A.M. We left the house at 5:30. I had only been in Pasadena once before, to buy textbooks for a course at UCLA. We crept along a foggy freeway to arrive at the Huntington Medical Foundation, located in an industrial park, at 6:30. We waited for ten minutes before my appointment and then walked into the building. The staff had just arrived and they were not ready for me. After a half hour, I entered the cylinder of the huge MRI machine, built by General Electric. When I was inside, I felt as though someone were banging a hammer on a steel garbage can. The basics of the sound-wave imaging had already been explained to me by the radiologist. Even though I found the noise irritating, I understood what it was.

Divina and I left the foundation by eight and drove back to her uncle's house. The next day, the UCLA neurologist called and said the MRI had turned up nothing abnormal. He could not tell me what had happened. He asked me to go to the University of Southern California neurology clinic, located in Good Samaritan Hospital, near downtown Los Angeles. That same morning I went to Good Samaritan, where I was directed to the neuromuscular disease clinic. The light there was fluorescent and intense, with attendant noise from the long tubes. The waiting room's temperature was super-air-conditioned, about sixty-five, and I was very uncomfortable. My wife filled out the patient information and medical insurance sheets. I was called into the clinic by a neurology fellow, a Pakistani man, dressed in strange balloon pants. Every resident and fellow seemed to be Pakistani.

I had bad feelings about the clinic from the start. I never had a high impression of the University of Southern California (USC). Perhaps this attitude derived from having attended UCLA. With the foreign medical graduates, the cramped clinic quarters, the overbright lighting, and the cruel air-conditioning, my impression of USC as a second-choice school was confirmed. When the Pakistani trainee told me he wanted to do a muscle biopsy, I decided it was time to get up and get dressed. He went to the clinic's attending physician, his boss, and told him I was leaving. The attending physician tried to change my mind. I told him I could not understand the trainee's English. He offered to take over my case. I declined. I had an overwhelming urge to leave the clinic and hospital. I entered the waiting room and got my wife and went out to the parking lot. We drove to her uncle's house. I was very upset.

The next day, Friday, I called the friendly UCLA neurologist and related my bad experience at the USC clinic. He apologized and said, "I don't know what to tell you. I cannot figure out what is wrong with you. I am sorry. Maybe you should go to the neuromuscular diseases clinic at the University of California, San Francisco" (UCSF). I asked if I had to go right away or if I could return to the Philippines and finish my work (I had three months left there). He told me I could go back to Manila and finish my work. He urged me to get in touch with UCSF as soon as I finally returned to Hawaii.

We flew to Honolulu, picked up my two children from my first marriage, Adrienne and Terrence, and took them to Manila for three months. I wrapped up my work and gave some seminars in Manila universities. The rest of the time was occupied with showing the children the Philippines and going on many trips. My health remained an unsettled issue and my body continued to lose muscle mass. I was worried.

Canal House

In mid-August, the four of us returned to Honolulu. The day before our flight, I got some type of flu. I had a fever and started to vomit. I felt miserable as we boarded the plane. When we arrived back in Hawaii, I still had a high fever and terrible congestion. My sister picked us up and drove us to our rental house on a canal leading to the ocean. The home belonged to a chemistry professor and his wife, who had gone on sabbatical in Europe.

The next day my sister and my wife took me to the family practitioner we shared with my sister's family. The physician told me I had pneumonia and admitted me to the local hospital in Kailua. The suspicion was that I had contracted some exotic tropical disease in the Philippines and I was put in an isolation room. I had a tropical medicine consult and many tests.

While I was lying in the hospital bed the most troubling thing was the constant twitching of my muscles. The more I worried about my condition, the more frequent and deep the twitching became. I complained to my family-medicine practitioner about the constant and irritating activity in my muscles. I could not rest. My body could not turn off, I felt. The doctor said he would send me to a neurologist.

I was discharged after a week. I took oral antibiotics. I felt exhausted and spent a week sleeping. When I was rested, I called the physician for the referral to the neurologist. My appointment was at five in the morning, his normal time for seeing patients. The diagnosis was motor neuron disease, or amyotrophic lateral sclerosis. (My visit to the neurologist is described in full in Chapter 2.)

I went home with the news that I had a fatal disease and could not expect to see the end of 1988. I cried a lot with Divina, always contemplating death and what it would mean to her and to my two children. We would spend hours in the darkest part of the house, crying and talking. After awful periods of sadness and depression, the two of us began to think of reading the research literature on motor neuron disease. My wife suggested we look for a new physician. I left it to her. We found Steven Berman, a decidedly East Coast Jewish internist. He has been my doctor and agent for twelve years.

I feel very comfortable with Berman. It is a matter of area cultural affinity, faith in his medical expertise, and his interactional style, in which he is always my agent and never my moral judge. I grew up in Great Neck, Long Island, an upper-middle-class suburb of New York City. The town was 80 percent Jewish, as were 95 percent of my friends. Although not a Jew, I felt comfortable with the New York Jewish culture, regarding it as my home culture. I was at ease with Berman, even with how he expressed anger. My Filipino wife would sometimes have reservations about my doctor's style and anger, however.

Berman is widely regarded as one of the best communicable diseases specialists in Hawaii. Most of his patients are referrals. He sees them in the morning only. Highly trained, Berman came to the state when the University of Hawaii opened its medical school. He was one of the founding members of the Department of Tropical Medicine. Although no longer a full-time faculty member, he still does research, publishes, attends research meetings, and teaches medical students and residents.

The best things about Berman are his capacity to act as your agent and his ability to make you think you are worth something, no matter how sick and disabled you may be. If you cannot get in to see a specialist, Berman will step in, make the call, and obtain the timely appointment. He will speak directly to the physician you want to see. The greatest of his skills is that having a life-threatening illness makes no difference in how Berman regards you. As Divina has pointed out, when you carry a life-threatening diagnostic label lesser doctors and health workers "see you as a dead man walking."

My favorite story about Berman is one often told by inpatient nurses, who complain about his aggressive treatment of infectious diseases in elderly patients. Many of them have serious degenerative diseases and are perceived as being near the end of life. I smile when I hear these stories, thinking it is the height of conceit for nurses or anyone else to decide to go lightly on therapy, hoping the patient will meet his or her end.

After we found Berman and established a working relationship with him, I decided to go to the University of California, San Francisco, medical center to follow up on the referral of the UCLA neurologist. I also consulted several colleagues from my days in the Department of Pediatrics and Human Development at Michigan State University. My former chairman there, Bill Weil, set up an appointment with the chief of the neuromuscular diseases clinic at UCSF. The chief of the clinic said, upon meeting us, "If I cannot figure out what is wrong with you, no one can." My wife and I were impressed by the self-confidence of this man in his early sixties. When we had a break from the diagnostic tests and examinations, we went to the campus bookstore and discovered our neurologist had just published a standard textbook on neuromuscular diseases.

I was examined and every bodily fluid was extracted and analyzed. After a spinal puncture, a high number of white cells were found in the spinal fluid, atypical for motor neuron disease. I had another MRI and was told, "You have a big brain." When the tests were completed, I was called into a small conference room, where the chief of the clinic summed up the tests and gave me his clinical assessment and prognosis. He said I had a kind of atypical motor neuron disease. He asked for permission to send my records to the University of Pennsylvania for review by a close colleague. He wanted to have his friend confirm his diagnosis.

It was then October 1985. The chief informed us that I would continue to get weaker. He said I would eventually lose my power to speak and even to walk. He said I would have strange mood swings, something that never happened, and that I would live out my life in a wheelchair, something that seems to be happening. He was vague about the long-term prognosis, telling us to call him as the disease progressed.

When Divina and I were in San Francisco, Harold Garfinkel accompanied us. As we wandered the halls of the medical center, we engaged in nonstop conversation, making the time and the sense of dread pass. Harold Garfinkel and his wife, Arlene, have been a constant source of help and encouragement in health crises.

We returned to Hawaii and resumed our life in the rented house on the canal. Because we were not ready to accept the San Francisco diagnosis, we focused on the irregular findings, contradictive of the diagnosis of motor neuron disease.

I went back to teaching and writing grants for mental health training in the Pacific Islands. My wife obtained a full-time teaching position in the Department of Nursing at Kapiolani Community College. We bought an additional car.

Our life was consumed by academic work on the weekdays and by visits from my two children on the weekends. We lived a normal life, making sure to get home in time to watch *Miami Vice*. But I grew gradually weaker, especially in the legs. I experienced some difficulty in speaking. I had some spells of vertigo (to be described in Chapter 2). I had some spectacular falls, once in the driveway, into a flower bed laden with peat moss, and once into the street in front of my sister's house. I fell one or two times on campus while walking to and from class.

I encountered an old girlfriend in front of the faculty mailboxes. I consciously put my right arm behind my back. My arm had suffered an enormous loss of muscle and was about half the size it was before the illness. She asked me about my arm and told me she had heard I had been sick. With some embarrassment, I showed her my atrophied arm. She told me it looked like a serious illness and asked if I wanted her sister, a local nurse, to find me an appropriate physician.

At the end of our year in the rental house, my children and their mother informed us that they were leaving Hawaii and moving to Fresno, California. This was and is a crushing blow—I never anticipated the separation from my children. Looking back, I realize I was quite naïve. My former wife was never happy in Hawaii, saying it was too hot. She could not get the kind of job she wanted. Plus, she was from California and wanted to return. When the Fresno schools offered her a teaching position, she quickly accepted.

Before my kids left for California, we had a weeklong visit from Harold Garfinkel. We had many long, intense conversations. It was an enjoyable time. But while Harold was here, I had my first experience with aspirating my food. We had gone to a Filipino restaurant and I swallowed some rice that went into my lungs. I had the worst coughing fit of my life. It was embarrassing and worrying. It was not to be the first aspiration. I would develop pneumonia from later ones.

In anticipation of the family who owned our rental house returning from sabbatical, Divina and I began to look for another place to rent in Kailua. Even though my kids were leaving, we wanted to remain in Kailua. It was much quieter than Honolulu, and all my children's friends lived there. I wanted them to have ready access to friends when they visited.

Hill House

We found a four-bedroom rental on a hill, with a view of the mountains. We moved in with the help of Larry Foster, a friend from Michigan. He was the first guest in our new house. We moved in July, after a vigorous campaign of cleaning up the house we were leaving. My sister came over and helped. I was not much use, as my right arm had lost strength. I could not move the arm, either.

The first event in the hill house was the arrival of my wife's parents from Manila. Divina had petitioned the United States Immigration and Naturalization Service for them when she became a naturalized citizen of the United States. We had been expecting them, and, as my condition grew worse, it became obvious that they could help us. My mother-in-law, Lourdes Telan, has been a tireless household worker, doing the laundry, cleaning the windows, and gardening. Lourdes cannot be idle. She cooks, as well.

In September 1986 we had a visit from Carleton Gajdusek, the Nobel Prize winner mentioned at the beginning of this chapter. He came with five boys from Papua New Guinea he had adopted. My friend Don Rubenstein, who had worked with Gajdusek in the Pacific Islands, was at the house as well. We spent the afternoon discussing my health and the Pacific Islands. Gajdusek kept admiring the view of the adjacent Koolau Mountains, comparing it to some vista in Tahiti.

We next had a visit from my former department chairman at Michigan State University, Bill Weil, and his wife, Vee. Things did not work out, because she found our house too hot and started to feel faint. We called my brother, Bob, who was then the engineer at the Sheraton Moana Surfrider Hotel and put them up in an air-conditioned room.

I had lost my ability to speak and we had developed a lip-reading system. (It is described in several chapters of this book.) We had to use the system, put together by my wife and my student research assistants, to talk to Weil and Gajdusek. I had used it at work and in teaching for about three months.

I was still sleeping in my queen size, normal bed with my wife. I had to have help in getting out of bed and in turning over. Sometimes I experienced moments of vertigo when trying to get out of bed. To make it easier for me to get into and out of bed, a woman gave us a wooden bed frame that raised the bed.

I started to experience difficulties eating and managing my posture at the kitchen table. Someone had to feed me, usually my mother-in-law. We had to get towels to pack on either side of my butt, to buff up my posture. I used to read the morning newspaper while packed this way into my office chair.

I could still walk. But it was getting more difficult. I had some spectacular falls, once scraping my head on the cheap rug in the family room. I had a big scab from the fall and everyone asked me what had happened.

I was grateful for the help of Deane Neubauer in teaching my classes, now that I had lost my voice. I describe Deane's assistance later in this book.

We stayed in the hill house until February 1988. By then I had lost the capacity to walk safely. I finally relented and got into a wheelchair. My wife thought I was in denial and would not use it for a host of reasons. I gave up driving at the same time as I began to use the wheelchair.

The best thing that happened in the hill house was my wife's pregnancy and the birth of our son, Thomas, on October 26, 1987. I was present at his birth. Tom has turned out to be a loving, model child.

After Tom was born, Divina and I started to think about buying a house. We had been paying rent for years and had no tax deductions and no capital appreciation. With advice from friends, we made the decision to buy. We had some savings, largely derived from the sale of my mother's house after she died. We would use this for the down payment.

Our House

My wife was looking ahead. She wanted to buy a house in a good elementary-school district. She researched the Stanford Achievement Test scores for each school in the Kailua area. We looked at about fifty houses and made an offer on one. We were beat out by another buyer. We were depressed, but then we found a house just in the area we wanted. We noticed a for-sale sign moments after it was put out.

This time, my wife and I were successful in our bid. We were attracted to the house because it was wheelchair friendly, having only one story, and because it was a newer, modern, double-wall structure. We moved in quickly, with the assistance of my brother and sister. Our new house was a block away from a good elementary school.

We went to San Francisco to give a paper at the American Sociological Association meetings in August 1989. Deane Neubauer met us in the city. The two of us had coauthored the paper and he would read it before the ethnomethodology session. It was the first time I had been away from Hawaii in three years. I not only attended the meetings but also visited my relatives in the San Francisco Bay area and went to Stanford Medical School for a last workup.

I had not yet given up reading the medical research literature on motor neuron disease. I was fascinated with the thesis that the disease was triggered by an immunological breakdown. Through Bill Weil, my former chairman in pediatrics at Michigan State, I set up neurological and immunological consults at Stanford. After the sociology meetings, we drove down to the university's medical center.

The consult was routine in neurology. The immunology physicians could not come up with anything. I was disappointed. However, after the visit to Stanford my wife and I had a long dialogue about running around, spending lots of time and money, looking for a proper name and a treatment for my condition. We decided we were focusing on a hoped-for treatment, instead of moving on with our life. Eventually, I would toss out my large files of copied journal articles on motor neuron disease. Years later, I would find I did not have time for the ALS newsletter on the Internet.

We returned to Hawaii with a sense of relief. We had decided we would just have to live with my condition.

Medical Crisis

At Easter 1991 I had my second bout of pneumonia. It started out as a cold but quickly grew worse. I had a hard time expectorating the phlegm. I went to the emergency room at Queen's Hospital and met my doctor there. I was hospitalized on a normal acute care unit, which turned out to be part of a pediatric unit. The hospital was full and had space for me only in pediatrics.

I was put on antibiotics. I enjoyed the nurses assigned to me. I had a long, funny dialogue with a Native Hawaiian nurse's aide. I was feeling slightly better and my doctor started talking about sending me home. Divina took sharp issue with this plan. My pneumonia had tired her out. She was not ready to take me home and insisted that I was not ready to go, either. Looking back, it is very evident that my wife knows my body better than anyone.

After a huge argument with my physician, joined by our best man, a local psychiatrist, I was discharged. On the ride home, I felt as if the cold and pneumonia were getting worse. I was home for a day or two and encountered great difficulty breathing. Divina called an ambulance. Unfortunately, no ambulance was available; fortunately, two firemen came to the house in a hook and ladder truck. They took one look at me and called back to the firehouse with the word that I would not last long. An ambulance finally arrived, and a Native Hawaiian fireman carried me out in his arms. My wife got in the front seat and the emergency technician started to put a plastic tube down my nose and throat. He attached an ambubag and started to pump air into my lungs. The technician kept telling me, "Hang on." I remember looking out the window, noticing the familiar landscape of the Pali Highway go by, and thinking that if I kept recognizing the features of the highway I would stay alive.

I was rushed into Queen's Hospital emergency room, about twenty miles from my house. Queen's is near downtown Honolulu and is the largest hospital in the state. It is the main teaching center for the University of Hawaii medical and nursing schools. Berman also practices there, and this is why I requested to be brought to Queen's, passing two other hospitals on the way.

The experience in the emergency room is a blur. I only remember the doctors re-intubating me and suctioning quarts of yellow liquid out of my lungs. I remember one resident remarking, "How can he hold so much liquid in his lungs and still be alive?" I was in a semiconscious haze as they worked on me. The only clear memory was from my first room in the intensive care unit (ICU).

I was put on a ventilator there. When I awoke from the drugs I had been given to relax me, I saw a smiling ICU male nurse. He called my wife into the room. It was very difficult to talk, as I had a ventilator tube down my right nostril and tape across my face to hold the tube in place. Divina went over what had happened in the emergency room. She said I was in serious shape and asked me not to die. I never thought of dying, at least not then. Thoughts of dying, particularly as a preferable alternative, would only come with the torture of the rocking bed, designed to break up phlegm in my lungs.

I would be in the ICU for months. I remember asking my wife to sleep in the room. I was very afraid my inability to talk would lead to a disaster, even my death. This foreboding would turn out to be true, in that I had many ICU nurses who inadvertently covered my trache when I was breathing room air. I have never had a home health care nurse who has not mistakenly covered this tube that runs down my windpipe. Usually, I have to struggle to get the nurses' attention by shaking my body, as much as I can; once they are aware of me, I cannot seem to indicate my trache is blocked and that I cannot breathe. Since my stay in the ICU and getting a trache, I make sure someone is with me who can lip-read. The reactions of the nurses who block my trache is either anger, telling me I am overreacting to not being able to breathe, or uncontrollable bouts of crying. The ones who cry say, "I almost killed him."

In my three months in the hospital my wife would spend the night 90 percent of the time; research assistants, colleagues, graduate students, or private nursing assistants would be with me the rest of the time. I continued to work during my stay in the ICU through the grace of my research assistants, particularly Andrea Leung. The help of this humorous young Chinese woman from Costa Rica would permit me to publish a book on social change in the Pacific Islands without delay. Some other research assistants had a hard time seeing me so sick and disabled, a few fainting as soon as they entered my room. They hit the floor and needed medical attention. (My time in the ICU is covered fully in Chapter 3.)

Upon my release from the hospital Divina was still working as a nursing instructor at Kapiolani Community College. During the day, I was left in the care of registered nurses from a home health care agency. They were either the best the profession had to offer or awful, with no one in between. One ICU nurse, who had just moved back to Hawaii from Texas, was the most skilled nurse I have ever had. I am proud she graduated from the University of Hawaii School of Nursing. She was pretty and friendly, too. On the other hand, I had a male nurse from abroad who repeatedly asked me if I thought I would be better off dead. I hated him and asked that he be replaced.

After a summer of home care my wife decided to resign from the faculty and support my return to work. She figured out that it would cost more than her income from teaching to hire nursing care for me during the day. I made more than Divina, and it was logical that she chose to protect my income. In the bargain I gained a meticulous nurse, who provides a depth of care unavailable from a rent-a-nurse. Plus, she is someone who I can discuss my work with.

When I returned to the university I was very weak. Moreover, I was worried about the substance, theoretical foundation, and future of my teaching, research, and writing. After three or four months I found I was not sweating and trembling so much. I had regained the strength I had before the hospitalization.

Return to Work

I faced two issues when I went back to the university. The first was the direction of my work. I had become a Pacific Islands researcher. Now, I found I could not travel to the islands and my access to research materials had been cut off. It would take some time to find a new direction. The other problem was reestablishing my staff of research assistants. Three of them had graduated while I was in the hospital, and I had only one person to work with. But Andrea Leung, one of the graduates, volunteered to work without pay until I had hired replacements. Andrea and Jennifer Spector interviewed dozens of candidates and came up with outstanding people to staff the office. I hired three new persons and said goodbye to Andrea, who moved to San Francisco.

I had started to talk to Divina about my experiences in the hospital, using ethnomethodology to frame them. My wife was familiar with this frame of analysis and knew and liked its founder, Harold Garfinkel. I used ethnomethodology not because it was a useful paradigm, one among many theoretical models, but because I was convinced that it alone addressed the concerted, bodily accomplishment of ordinary tasks, such as caregiving. Most of the troubles I encountered with nurses were due to my not being able to talk. I could not build the sequence of care with them through speech. It was ethnomethodology that focused on this phenomenon.

My wife started to urge me to do two things. The first was to write about my illness. The second was to return to what she called my "roots": ethnomethodology. She had been hearing about these roots from the day she met me. Ethnomethodology, and particularly Harold Garfinkel, are not just another college course and instructor. The discipline and the man cast a lifelong spell.

It was not that easy to return to ethnomethodology. I still had a number of commitments to write papers about the Pacific Islands. I had a large, successful seminar on social change in the islands. I had a book under way on social change in Hawaii. I found it emotionally difficult to write about my illness.

I overcame the reluctance to get back into ethnomethodology. First, a friend at the University of Oregon, Ken Liberman, asked me to write a paper for a conference. I tried to write a postmodern-theory essay on my experience in the ICU. I felt as if the paper were pure cant, empty of real empirical reference. Struggling with the materials for it, I found myself going back to ethnomethodology as a natural event. I also had the consistent encouragement of my wife and my sociologist friend in Toronto, John O'Neill. He kept telling me the work was my own and I should not worry about what anyone said.

Present

From 1992–93 I telescope to the time I write this, late October 1997.

I have continued my career as a professor of sociology at the University of Hawaii. Except for my hospitalization, I have never missed a day of work (until, after October 1997, my wife was hospitalized and going to the university was out of the question for a short time). Work is my primary means of fulfillment. I have been aided by a wonderful chain of research assistants. These students are more than my arms, fingers, and legs—they are an important source of emotional strength for me and my wife. I have kept in touch with those research assistants who have graduated.

Another source of support has been Dick Post and his wife, Janet. I met Dick in the dorm cafeteria at UC Berkeley, in line at the milk dispenser. We started talking about how nice it was that students could drink as much milk as they wanted. We became close friends, often spending wild weekends with girls in Big Sur, California. Both of us went on to graduate school. Later, I took my first job at Michigan State University, and Dick became an assistant professor of physics at the University of Wisconsin. He drove over to Michigan many times to visit. We were on the phone weekly.

After I moved to Hawaii, I lost contact with him. I did not know he had moved to MIT. One day, about three years ago, Dick called our house. Divina talked to him, describing the divorce from my first wife, how she and I then met in Micronesia, our marriage, where my first two kids were, my illness, and my continued work as a professor. The conversation took hours. Soon, Dick arrived in Honolulu. He was on his way to a conference in Japan. He stayed with us and brought us up to date on his life, including the fact that he had started his own business.

I mention Dick here because he is the most positive, optimistic person I have met. He has become an important friend of the whole family. My son calls him for advice on his science projects. Although Dick lives outside Boston, it seems as if he were a next-door neighbor. He has assisted us in many ways. Now he is a full-time businessman, having resigned his faculty position at MIT.

As I conclude this narrative of my illness, my wife has been diagnosed with breast cancer. Surgery is scheduled for next week. We have marshaled our friends and family to take care of me while she is going through treatment. The trauma of the situation is a clear demonstration of Divina's centrality in my care and in my ability to work; it also points to her role as the hub of the entire extended family. Again, my student assistants and former assistants have come to play an important role in my care, coming to my house and helping out while my wife is having treatment. Dick Post has been instrumental in getting the help together, and he and his wife will come out shortly after the surgery.

Story Telling

I could have told this story of my illness in many ways. I have actually told it differently in the past. I will tell it differently in the future. But, this time, I have had a long turn at talk, over thirty pages of typescript. This narrative is longer than what I could possibly enunciate in a whole afternoon of speaking. Also, this is a written narrative, very different from the interactional sensitivities of conversation.

The written narrative has certain emergent features. One of them is that once you start writing you develop themes. Some of these have to be extended, to give substance to earlier statements. When you start writing these extensions, you both give examples of earlier general statements and discover that you have developed central themes without noticing it. Thus it is with this narrative: the progressive nature of my illness; my wife, Divina; my graduate school teacher, Harold Garfinkel; and my student assistants have become the central characters. I could have, and have, told my story with different central characters and not proved this telling untrue.

2 You Are Lucky Your Wife Stuck with You

When I was in the intensive care unit of Hawaii's largest hospital, the nurses were constantly telling me to be "a good boy." These requests were so frequent that they seemed like demands. I was in such a miserable state, with a breathing tube stuck down my nose and throat and with massive bandages on my nose to hold the tube in place, that I ignored the "good boy" talk.

After I had a tracheotomy and the bandages were removed, I began to pick up the meaning of being "a good boy." Nurses would tell me that I had been "a good boy" after a night of uninterrupted sleep. I heard them talking outside my door, saying Mr. D was "a bad boy," "keeping us up all night with calls." On another day the nurses were chatting by my door, complaining about Mr. W., who "gave us a hard time." They further remarked, "We had to work on him all night long. He is a bad patient." When the same bunch of nurses entered my room, they said, "Don't be like Mr. W. Be a good boy. Don't call us too much."

I began to get the drift. I started to ask what this talk about being "a good boy" meant. The nurses told me being "a good boy" or good patient means not requiring a lot of time and attention. I asked, through a lip-reading student translator, "What are you here for, if not to deliver bedside care?" The reply was: "We have some very serious patients here and we have to work on them a lot. If people are calling us to their rooms all the time, we will not have enough time to work on the serious patients."

I pushed my inquiry further. How many patients, I asked the nurses, were they responsible for in the intensive care unit? "Each nurse has two patients," they told me. I asked, "If each nurse has only two patients, why are you worried about patients requiring too much time?" One of them answered, "When a patient is really bad, sometimes we all have to work on him." I asked how often this happens. The response was, "Often, and we never know when we will have a bad patient or when a patient will start to go down the tubes." When I reported I could see how much time they spent at the nursing station, eating, chatting, and doing paperwork, I was told, "We have to be free to respond to emergency situations." When I sarcastically inquired, "Is 'being a good boy' leaving you free to eat doughnuts?" the response was, "This is stressful work, we see a lot of death here. We need down time and this allows us to recharge and get ready for the next bad patient. Not everyone is like you. Most of our patients are unconscious."

Motivated Illness

What does it mean to be a "good boy"? It means to be a patient who does not express symptoms requiring the attention of a nurse. Such reasoning trades on an assumption that patients have some motivational control of their symptoms, or at least should have.

I doubt that nurses, as individuals, would seriously argue for this notion of motivational control over illness. If confronted with tape recordings of their words, they would, I suspect, dissociate themselves from such views, saying it was "just nurse talk." However, the conversational descriptors or moral labels of "good patient," "bad patient," and "good-boy patient" were always there during my hospitalization. I suspect that they may be omnipresent in nursing work.

When I had been discharged from the intensive care unit and was about to go home, three nurses, standing in the hallway near the automatic door, yelled out to me and Divina, "Britt, don't give your wife much trouble. Be a good boy." When I visit the emergency room of the same hospital, the respiratory therapists who know me from my inpatient experience will ask my wife, "Has he been a good boy?" A different version of this rhetoric can be found in another question respiratory therapists direct at my wife: "Has he been giving you a hard time?" Even Divina will ask the nurses we hire for Saturday respite care, "Did he give you a hard time?"

The late American sociologist Talcott Parsons (1978) said one of the properties of the sick role was being exempt from responsibility. This exemption includes responsibility for the present illness. I think this theoretical position, which no one would argue with on logical grounds, is at odds with the way normal people talk in the course of the day. The discrepancy between sociological theory and social reality is a recurrent problem. As Garfinkel (1996) has pointed out, sociology is a constructive analytic science, otherwise called formal analytic, based on idealizations of society, which ignores naturally occurring interactions, including conversation.

It is plain that sociology, at least constructive analytic or hypothetico-deductive sociology, has adopted the commonsense cultural position that talk, especially that occasioned in conversation, is just talk, unreliable, an epiphenomenon of social structure. The actual doing of nurses, talking the rhetoric of motivated illness, is not observed. Talk is, though, the very material by which social structure is produced and reproduced. Nurses have many other ways of talking—as we all do—but the moral attributions of controlling your symptoms and the corresponding need for care is a frequent or even prevailing way of talking. Some might be horrified at this rhetoric, expecting a more professional, neutral form of speech, but it is unrealistic to expect to talk outside commonsense culture. I take it that this form of talk existed before any of the current nurses on the intensive care unit arrived and that it is seen as a rational way of preserving, by conversational formulation, their allocation of time to specific tasks. Nurses new to the unit fit themselves to this preexisting fashion.

Contrary to Parsons, there is no escaping role expectations in major illnesses and in chronic disease. The sick, instead of being allowed to suffer in quiet, are addressed with supposed reasons they have become sick—for example, "You could not control your eating and drinking." For the chronically ill, the comments will often be directed at how the person is a burden, requiring constant care; some remarks will be directed at the cost of care; and a few formulations will focus on the person's lack of will, as seen in the comment directed at an individual having trouble standing —"What is wrong with you, why don't you stand up?"

I may appear to have a dim view of nurses. I make many negative comments about them in this book. My observations are focused on the way they talk. I do not think nurses are unique in their dissociation from their talk. Casual talk, naturally occurring conversation, is universally considered "just talk." I love the power of the following formulation: "It is just talk. I didn't mean anything by it." Talk, especially talk in work settings, seems exempt from examination. It's only "shop talk." The implication is that shop talk is a second-order happening to the real order of the work site, in this case the intensive care unit.

Nurses are like everyone else in using common sense or the popular culture sense of illness in their casual conversation. When my brother showed up at my house with an alarming weight gain of forty pounds, I began to think of the likely reasons he could not control his appetite. My alarm was related to the heart attack he had two years ago. After he left, Divina and I discussed his weight gain, and we were joined in the conversation by my mother-in-law. One of the main categories in the interaction was control of eating and its relation to disease and symptoms. I eventually e-mailed my brother's wife and told her I was concerned about his health. We went over possible lifestyle changes and how they might lead to enhanced control over eating. What amount to moral attributions about control are conversationally common in regard to obesity, as they are about controlling symptoms in the intensive care unit.

I want to switch gears now and talk about a remark made to me and my wife. We were visiting the office of my gastroenterologist for a gastro-tube change. I am fed through a tube to avoid food getting into my lungs. After he had changed my tube and I had gotten down from the examination table and was sitting in my wheelchair, the doctor unleashed the following remark, without provocation: "You are lucky you have a wife who stuck by your side. Most people in your condition have had their wives split long ago." Divina immediately replied, facing me, "You see, you see!"

I was put off by the physician's unsolicited comment. I heard it not only for itself but for how it represented the awful weight of commonsense culture about paralyzed, chronically ill persons. I was aware of the late Senator Jacob Javits of New York, having motor neuron disease and going through an ugly divorce; I was aware, too, of many other wives divorcing their husbands because of chronic disability. I heard the remark of the physician as a left-handed endorsement of the commonsense reasoning that women married to disabled paralytic men should divorce them. I heard his remark as denigrating life with a paralyzed person. I heard my wife's response as referencing that body of commonsense reasoning.

Go Home and Take Valium and Get Counseling

After I returned from my Fulbright Professorship in Manila, I got terribly sick. I had sweating and chills on the flight back to Honolulu. When I landed and got home, I started to vomit. I had a fever and muscle aches. As I began to get sick the muscle twitches, called fasciculations, became more frequent and violent. I went to my family practitioner. He told me I had pneumonia and put me in a small community hospital. I was assigned an isolation room because they thought I might have brought back some exotic tropical disease from the Philippines. They tested me for everything, but seemed to focus on leptospirosis, a disease caused by animals, often rats. I had an infectious disease specialist consult, and he ruled out leptospirosis.

I got better within a week and was discharged. On a follow-up visit to the doctor, he noticed muscular atrophy and the constant fasciculations. He referred me to a neurologist. This doctor practiced at what was then an exclusive private hospital; he kept strange hours and agreed to see me at five in the morning. I arrived at the hospital while it was very dark and checked in with the outpatient coordinator. The hospital office was empty, except for one outpatient clerk.

I found the neurologist dressed in hospital scrubs. Unlike the other neurologists I had met and would meet, this local Japanese man appeared to be very athletic, with well-developed arms. His manner was nonchalant. He breezily hooked me up to an electromyograph machine. While he was testing the electrical conduction of my muscles he received a personal telephone call. With pins stuck through my skin to points in the muscles, and a small charge coursing from one needle to the other through my muscles, he talked to his friend about chartering a fishing boat for a trip to the Kona Coast of the island of Hawaii. I quickly became annoyed.

After he finished the test, he said, "We have to talk." No sooner had he uttered this than he received a call from the same friend. They spent another ten minutes talking about the fishing trip. My anxiety grew and I started to sweat. When he was finished on the phone, he turned toward me, walked four steps, heaved a big, pensive sigh, and told me, "You have ALS, or Lou Gehrig's disease." He went on, "Most people who have ALS, or amyotrophic lateral sclerosis, live three years from diagnosis." I commented, "It is a fatal disease." He replied, "It does not hurt, like cancer." I asked, "Is there any treatment?" He said, "No." He said, "We have to take a muscle biopsy to see if I am right in my diagnosis and to see, if we can, how far along you are." "How long do I have?" I asked. "I would not bank on anything beyond 1988," he answered.

I was devastated by his diagnosis and, even more, by his seemingly calculated breeziness. When he pressed me to make an appointment for the muscle biopsy, I told him, "I am very busy at work and I will have to make room in my schedule. I can't make a commitment now. I will call you."

Beginning to sense my personal dislike for him, he answered, "Do as you like."

That whole day, and on into the evening, Divina and I discussed what a horrible creature the neurologist had been. The next day we went to the family physician who had made the referral. By the time we got to his office we had our complaint lines down. When the doctor came into the room, we pounced. "The neurologist was an asshole, more interested in talking on the phone with a friend about the weekend's fishing trip to Kona than talking to us." My wife said, "We didn't like his manner. He was awful." Our family doctor nodded in acknowledgment but pointed out, "I know his news was hard to take but he is a very well trained neurologist and is held in high regard by most doctors." I replied, "I don't care what anyone thinks of him, he is a super asshole. He treated us like dogs."

The family practitioner drew his clasped hands to his mouth, indicating deep thought. After this noticed pause, the doctor said, "I don't want to deal with the neurologist. I want to talk about how the Robillards are going to deal with a fatal disease." We nodded. He went on, "You have to get a psychologist. You will have bad and good days but you will have to deal with the inevitable end. The psychologist will help you prepare for the end. I will help you relax by giving you Valium. The Valium will help with muscle stiffness and spasms and it will adjust your mood."

I said, "You sound just as bad as the other guy." He responded, "This is serious stuff and I don't think we can deny it." I suddenly realized the book was already written for this doctor and there were no more pages to the story. With head gestures, I indicated to Divina that it was time to leave.

It would be easy to criticize both physicians for having poor patient communication. What I want to address, though, is how such seemingly uncaring statements can be made as a matter of course and, moreover, how they can be made without preparing the patient.

It delights me to no end to be writing this book twelve years after the family practitioner and the neurologist told me I had three years to live. What the family practitioner did, in his statements, was to present me and my wife with a close horizon, a lesser form of existence, denigrated by illness and a prognosis of death. There is something about having a fatal disease, an officially diagnosed fatal illness, that immediately renders the diagnosee less worthy, and having fewer prospects, than others. This image of the life of the fatally ill leads to comments like the physicians telling me to go home, take Valium, get death counseling, and prepare to die. The family practitioner is hardly alone in his assumptions about people who are fatally ill. It is a social text, shared by most people in society and reproduced in their remarks.

There is an alternative text that says one lives until one dies, but one does not hear it much. When the patient does hear this formulation—that life is not over until it is over—it can sound like it is being introduced as a corrective to the negative view of terminally ill individuals.

Vertigo

My major muscles started to atrophy when we got back from the Fulbright Professorship in Manila in the fall of 1985. Divina and I had rented a three-bedroom house from a chemistry professor who was on sabbatical. I noticed I was having increasing trouble walking and standing. I would often stumble over the front of my feet; I could not pick them up nor could I pick up my toes. I suffered a big fall when I got out of my car one evening and fell, face first, into the flower bed. Fortunately, it was filled with peat moss and I received only a few scratches. The other fall was in the street, in front of my sister's house. Again, I fell face first, but this time it was against pavement. I received numerous cuts to my face.

The loss of the ability to extend and lift the front of my feet and the falls were precursors to the loss of muscle fibers throughout my body. Actually, this atrophy must have been going on for a long time, but it was at this moment that movement became a problem. I started to experience difficulty in spatial orientation as I walked near walls. I became dizzy as I labored to get around in the kitchen, having trouble using my arm movements for balance, using my back muscles to remain upright, and moving my legs and feet in a coordinated way. The sought-for movements, which had once, unnoticed, produced stability, were no longer there. I would step or reach, oriented toward specific points. Instead of getting to them with ease, I would shake, often going into spasms, and the acts of movement I had done millions of times became problematic. While I struggled to achieve the spatial points I had hardly noticed before, the room would begin to spin. Sometimes I would fall into the kitchen counters or into the washer and dryer.

Another incident of spatial problems and experienced vertigo came when I was trying to get out of bed. This occurred a year later, after we had moved out of the chemistry professor's house and into another rental house. I was still sleeping in our queen-size bed. It was a major struggle to get myself into a sitting position. My stomach muscles had weakened, and when I tried to sit up they would shake and often cramp. I quickly became aware of how central these stomach muscles are in coordinating the simultaneous movement of the legs and upper torso. I had great difficulty sitting up and moving my legs to the side of the bed, preparatory to standing. Soon, I stopped trying to sit up. I preferred to slide myself to the side of the bed and then, using my arms, try to sit up and swing my feet over the floor. However, the stomach muscles were still involved in sliding myself to the side, even more in sitting up and putting my legs over the edge. Grunting, perspiring, breathing in deep gulps, shaking, sometimes going into muscle spasms with painful cramps, I was rewarded with the violent rotation of the room. What had been an effortless act, getting out of bed, had become a monumental achievement. What I had done for over forty years, completely without notice, had become an obstacle. I became aware of movements and relationships between movements that had remained unconscious for many decades.

Balance and coordination, like conversation (perhaps a surprising analogy), are based on a prior understanding of a broad text of human behavior and its possibilities. The movement of each leg and arm, the head, and the trunk is based on, finds its precision of extension and contraction in, a long residue of previous movements. This residue is an unnoticed text of ordinary movements. Consider, for example, subconsciously guiding the extension of the leg just so many feet, the muscles and tendons that lift the front of the foot, the planting of the foot, the feet in the bottom of the foot, pushing the foot and leg back, both by bringing the other leg and foot forward and by using the muscles in the foot to push the foot back, and coordinating the upper body with the movements of the legs.

When I could no longer manipulate my body parts according to my historical residue of movement patterns, I realized I was reaching to move my legs, and roll my trunk, toward specific points, whether measured by weight distribution or by moving my body through space. When I first experienced these difficulties, I also often experienced vertigo. I was afraid I was having symptoms of yet another neurological disease. I started to inspect my life for physical and mental stressors that could lead to vertigo. After I got a wheelchair and ceased my Herculean efforts to move my body by myself, the bouts of vertigo became less frequent. After a year they finally stopped.

When I first accepted a wheelchair, I often thought the individual who was pushing was not paying attention and would wheel me off the curb, turning my wheelchair over and throwing me to the ground. Fortunately, there have been only four such accidents in the ten years since I stopped walking. When I first started using the wheelchair, curbs and uneven surfaces would whiz by, making me feel dizzy and out of control. But gradually I started to develop a new residue of experiences in the wheelchair, and the loss of spatial stability ceased to be a problem. Rooms no longer whirled. The landscape stayed in place.

The texts of remarks and bodily movements are subject to change. My experience with muscular atrophy and paralysis revealed the unnoticed assumptions guiding body movement and demonstrated that spatial stability is a bodily achievement. Achievement occurs when the coordinates of bodily movement residues meet. The experience of vertigo, and its gradual dissipation through building up a new set of residues, illustrates the relationship between underlying assumptions and the things that signify them, in this case utterances and movements. After some time in the wheelchair, the moment-to-moment experiences signified and verified a new set of residues about spatiality. I no longer became dizzy and the environment did not race around.

The same thing happens with the underlying texts of utterances. With time, the statements of physicians, including specialists, and the "blame the patient" rhetoric of the nurses, asking me to "be a good boy," were transcended. I not only lived through these textual residues but the repetitive nature of the references made me realize that these statements and underlying texts were standard figures of speech. Pretty soon, Divina and I could recognize many of these figures, and we came to regard them with ironic glee. We are no longer members of the seriousness of the text of wives leaving their disabled husbands. Time alone has allowed us to cast off the dreary—end of life—texts of the neurologist and family practitioner. We have not gotten past the "be a good boy" form of speech, because we continue to resist this kind of patient management.

3 Communicating in Intensive Care

Hospitalization in an intensive care unit is physically uncomfortable and socially disorganizing. The ordinary forms of conversational participation that generate and sustain a sense of agency are breached when the patient cannot communicate in socially consensual "real time." I, for example, had to use an alphabet board, a process that is slow enough to disrupt the rhythms of ordinary "real time" communication.

Monitors and Communication

I once set out to write a paper about monitor screens and the displacement of the person in the intensive care unit (ICU). I sometimes thought I had become like William Gibson's (1984) characterization of a human with cyborg parts. I had to look at the monitor screens to find out if I was alive, how close to death I was, and if I was making any progress toward recovery. The monitors were my constant focus when I was alone. They were, as well, the focus of those taking care of me. My heart rate was monitored, as were my blood pressure, respiration, the oxygen saturation level of my blood, the other blood gases, my temperature, urinary output, and the infusion rate of my medications; in the bargain, my prostrate body was monitored by a television camera in the ceiling. I lived in and by the collective scanning of the monitors by myself and by my caretakers.

Let me illustrate this point about living in the monitors. When ICU nurses would come into my room, they could flick a remote switch on their belt and the monitor readouts of other patients would be projected on my own monitor screen. That way a nurse could keep track of other patients while working in my room. I was at first unaware that my nurse routinely switched on my neighboring patient's readout on my monitor. I would look at and listen to "my" monitor and become alarmed at the falling blood pressure, the irregular cardiac rhythm, the low oxygen saturation level, and the bells and buzzers that would go off to signal the need for immediate, life-saving assistance. Thinking it was my readout, my blood pressure would jump to near 200, my respiration rate would increase to 40 per minute, my oxygen saturation level would sink into the 80s, and my own monitor alarm bells and buzzers would go off.

It was this confusion of living in monitor screens, whether your own or others' mistaken for such, that caught my analytic attention. I proposed to write about the displacement of the self by the screens, with the added dimension that the monitor screens were located in my room as well as at the nursing station, about a hundred feet away. The displacement was not only characterological, involving finding the truth about who you are in the screens, but spatial as well. Most of the monitor reading, so at least you thought and hoped, took place at the nursing station. The placement of careful and continuous reading of the monitors there may have been a panoptic dream, but it effectively removed the critical reading of factors concerning life and death, as well as televised bodily behavior, to a remote, unseen location. Additionally, the actions derived from this information were formulated in an invisible place, a site beyond personal influence.

When I started writing the paper on the monitor screens,

however, I compiled page after page on my communication problems with the nursing staff, physicians, and other workers on the hospital floor. I am afflicted with a neuromuscular disease, and I cannot talk or communicate in anything approaching the social consensus of "real time." I came to feel as if I had deserted my initial project of describing my uncomfortable journey in the cyberspace of the monitors. I faced a dilemma: either put aside the description of my communication problems or proceed with the theme of the monitor screens. The more I worked on the paper, the larger my failure at consensus "real time" communication loomed as the source of my discomfort in the ICU, even with the monitors. The direction of the paper seemed clearer, and I eventually came to see that the dislocating, self-distancing (Zola 1982) trouble with the monitors was not all that different from most nurses failing to use my alphabet board to talk with me. When I could not communicate, I had no participation in my care or the way I was regarded and the way I came to view myself.

The paper explicitly uses the self as the primary source of data. I long ignored this experience in doing sociology, feeling like Irving Zola (1982) must have when he wrote in the first paragraph of his book *Missing Pieces*, "Yet for over two decades I have succeeded in hiding a piece of myself from my own view." Even though I have suffered this illness since 1985 and have been in a wheelchair since 1988, I felt constrained from consulting this experience until I wrote the paper in 1993. I implicitly regarded personal experience as a "forbidden pool" of knowledge, one to be used but never acknowledged (Fine 1992). This diffidence about describing the experience of disability is shared by the late disabled anthropologist Robert Murphy (1987) in his book *The Body Silent*. In retrospect, such reluctance is strange for someone trained as an ethnomethodologist. The "unique-adequacy requirement" (Garfinkel 1986; Schutz 1967) for beginning a study of a social setting states that the analyst must be a recognized participant in the practices he or she is describing. Most authors of ethnomethodological studies, however, after assuring the reader they are proficient practitioner in the setting described, quickly turn to the third person. The use of the "I" as the subject of analysis is an embarrassment for many. It remained for Dorothy Smith (1987) to explicitly theorize the self as the source of analytical knowledge and as the subject of official research. I was encouraged to use the experience of my disability as a broad sociological topic by Irving Zola. He led a colloquium in Honolulu in the spring of 1993. In his talk and in personal conversation afterward, he used his disability to open up broad issues of social order, for both the able and the disabled.

The Illness

My paper was based on three and a half months of hospitalization, most of it in the ICU. The fieldwork is not recommended. I have had a neuromuscular disease since 1985, and an acute episode of pneumonia in 1991 brought me to the hospital in an ambulance. My lungs had filled up with fluid; I was having extreme difficulty breathing. The emergency medical service crew of the ambulance stuck a tube in my nose and down to my lungs and pumped air in with a bag. The pumping continued throughout the twenty-minute ride to the hospital. Attached to the bag was a cylinder of oxygen. When I arrived at the emergency room, I was rushed inside to a room where seven people began to work on me. I was reintubated: a new tube was stuck in my nose, down my throat, and into my lungs. The fluid was suctioned out of my lungs. This suctioning would become a permanent feature of life.

I cannot talk. I can communicate by forming individual letters with my lips. I could emit some vocal sounds before the hospitalization, but I did not have enough muscle strength and control to articulate words. I spoke by spelling out words by moving my lips. This is a slow process and does not match the "real time" order of natural conversation. Moreover, the number of persons who can read my lips is highly limited. My lip movements are restricted, due to weak lip muscles, and it takes intensive training and exposure to be able to understand me. The students who work for me as research assistants can read my lips, as can my wife, daughters, and mother-in-law. Otherwise, I have to communicate by using an alphabet board, an even slower process than lip reading. Most of the time when I was in the hospital I had to use the alphabet board with nurses, nurses' aides, and respiratory therapists. Occasionally, a student research assistant would work with me on a book, and for that time I could communicate more rapidly by lip movements. My wife, Divina, spent most nights with me in the room; she could read my lips and tell the staff what I was saying.

I found not having a "real time" voice equivalent to not having any defense against what was done to my body. Once my body was touched, I had no control over the intensity or the painful effects of a given procedure. I came to visualize having a voice as having the defense of making assertions about myself, making threats and counterthreats, and otherwise carving out and maintaining a space for myself. I could not control what was happening to my body, nor could I control the interactions that largely made up my person. I could not even communicate simple information about my condition to my doctors and most of my nurses. It was very difficult to gain people's attention and to hold it through the course of a conversation. The physicians, operating under tremendous time pressures, would limit their visits to my room to fifteen minutes, time enough for only a few, if any, of my laboriously formulated sentences. They would suggest that I formulate what I had to say before they came. This suggestion left out the possibility that I might want to participate in any emergent conversation while they were in the room. It also assumed that I would remember what I wanted to say in conversational contexts long after the conversation had passed. Some doctors made decisions in the room about treatment, including surgery, and I could not respond other than by giving a simple yes or no with head movements. It was impossible to give a qualified answer, and many times the physician would leave the room while I was trying to spell out a reply. Often, the doctor would not see himself as the recipient of my reply: the time lag was too great, and his attention had switched to a new task. Furthermore, the person interpreting what I was trying to say could become so concerned about reading my lips or using my alphabet board that she or he forgot to signal the physician that I was saying something to him.

Not being able to influence most aspects of my experience in the hospital by conversing generated frustrations and resentments. Others made attributions about my intelligence and my motivations; I, equally, made attributions about the intelligence, motivations, and sensitivity of my medical caregivers and about the irrationality of the entire health care delivery system.

Flying Nurses

The communication problem with most nurses was the same as with physicians. Most of those in the ICU were visiting nurses from the U.S. mainland. In my experience they were uniformly Caucasians, or *haoles,* as they are known in Hawaiian. These nurses call themselves "flying nurses"; they sign short-term contracts to work for from three months to a year. Most of them worked on three- to six-month contracts. Most worked three twelve-hour shifts each week and would have four days off to enjoy Hawaii. The hospital paid round-trip airfare from the mainland and subsidized their apartment rent. The flying nurses lived together in the same large apartment building (appropriately named the Marco Polo) and mainly socialized with each other. It is not too much to say that they lived a colonial-compound existence, like the British in India. Many of these caregivers had worked in ICUs in major medical centers on the U.S. mainland. The national need for intensive care nurses was so great that some were able to spend years working the circuit of resort areas in the United States.

It was my feeling the flying nurses were almost impossible to communicate with. I had a much easier time talking with their local counterparts. Unfortunately, the number of ICU nurses who permanently lived in Hawaii, whether they were immigrants or had been born and raised in the state, was small. The flying nurses knew little of the social structure, culture, and history of Hawaii. They knew the Hawaiian pidgin English word for urine (*shi shi*) and the Hawaiian word for finished (*pau*), but little else.

It was not by intention, but the flying nurses could not locate me in their conversations. The "me" they could locate was a generic person, but it was not the "me" that lived in Hawaii, had friends, worked, and had a history in Hawaii and the Pacific Islands. These nurses could talk about where they were from, where they had gone to nursing school, where they had worked, and where I had lived and worked on the U.S. mainland. But when the dean of the School of Nursing at the University of Hawaii would visit me, they did not recognize her. Clinical instructors in the School of Nursing met with the same response. (The local nurses, on the other hand, would quiz me about my relationship to nursing faculty.) When my research assistants would come to work with me, they had to fight being hurried out of the room. The flying nurses treated me as a standard sick person, someone too sick to be working and in no command of his circumstances. It seemed that they could not describe me except as a sick person equivalent to countless others in their experience.

Their denial of my individuality was connected to the alphabet board. None of them would use it. A few would try, but they would become frustrated and stop. The most common problem was that the nurses could not remember the letters of the words as I selected them from the alphabet board. They would not write the letters and words down. They would reverse letters, forget the last letter of the sequence, and quickly lose all sense of progression through words, sentences, and paragraphs. When we would move from the first word to the second and third, the first word would often be forgotten.

I discovered that even when most nurses correctly spelled out a word without writing it down they could not recognize the word, even after repeatedly saying each of its letters. I learned that spelling out words is not equivalent to recognizing them, especially among native speakers of English. This would happen both for short words ("what," "is," "the") and for longer words ("responsible," "routine," "medication," "procedure"). A nurse would stand before me and spell out W-H-A-T over and over again without recognizing it.

I had a hard time separating words, and many of my nurses would run them together, as in "Iwanttocallmywife." This was completely unintelligible. I got as lost as the nurses when they would spell out run-together words. I would have to start all over again. Separating words became a paramount problem. I would try to stop after spelling out a word to indicate its completion. But, as I came to learn, most persons could not recognize a word even after they had spelled it correctly and had repeated it several times. I would try jerking my head to the right to indicate a word had been completed, but I found that this was too easily mixed up with saying no by shaking my head from side to side. Indicating the stops between words was and is a continuing problem, even for those who write down the letters as I sequentially spell them.

Anticipating these communication troubles, most flying nurses would say, "I am not even going to try the board." Others would declare, "It is no sense in trying to communicate. I know what needs to be done and I am going to do it." A few would remark, "I have a job to do, so don't give me any trouble by trying to talk." The most memorable line came at a first encounter: "I am the nurse from hell and do not try any of that communication shit with me." The nurses seemed to think that working with a patient in my condition could be carried out without any communication. I was made aware that "most" patients in the ICU could not make themselves understood by any means and that I was taking critical time away from the care of others by using an inefficient communication process. There was a flutter of talk about outfitting me with a speech prosthesis, as if such an instrument would cure my communication problems. There was a naïve belief that a speech prosthesis would operate in the "real time" of normal conversation.* My insistence on talking and being heard, expecting what I said to influence behavior, led to a spiral of mutual antagonism between myself and the flying nurses. I came to think of them as nearly interchangeable parts, mirroring what I thought that they thought of their patients.

Local Nurses

I had more success with the few persons resident in Hawaii who served in the ICU. But it did not extend to all local nurses. Some of them are military dependents, working

*I know of no computer-assisted speech device that speaks in real time. I have made a thorough investigation of the synthesized-speech market.

here for three or four years and then moving on to a new assignment. Persons new to the state make up another, relatively small, portion of local nurses. They are usually Caucasian, dependents of business people or professionals who have just moved to Hawaii. A few of them have been recruited from the mainland. Military dependents and the newly arrived cannot be considered authentic local nurses.

What I mean by the term "local nurses" are persons either locally trained or longtime residents of Hawaii. They need not have been born and raised in the state. Many authentic local nurses are from the Pacific Islands and the Philippines or are Caucasians from the U.S. mainland who went to college in Hawaii. But most local nurses were born, raised, and educated here.

Authentic local nurses could—by glances, gaze, facial expression, vocabulary, syntax, cadence, dialect, body language, and topical reference—locate themselves and their patients as members of the same local culture and social structure. We could exchange information about neighborhoods, schools, places of employment, local and national cultures, food, and life histories, all in the context of Hawaii, or, in short, the formulation that we belonged to this place, something that pervades and appears essential in social interaction among local residents. For these nurses, I had an individual personality. There was a reciprocity of highly detailed knowledge that located both me and them: we knew each other as unique, situated individuals. We did not deal in generic, universal categories.

Not all local nurses could communicate with me. No male nurse so much as tried to use my alphabet board. (This is consistent with my experience outside the hospital. Males, in general, appear not to have the patience or the multiple communication rhythms to be able to use alternative means of communication.) On the other hand, three nurses and one respiratory therapist consistently used my alphabet board. One nurse was a local Chinese woman, whose first language was Cantonese. Although she spoke English without an accent, she spoke only Cantonese until entering elementary school. The second nurse was a Chamorro (a person of Micronesian, Spanish, and Filipino descent) from Guam, whose first language was Chamorro. The third was a Hawaiian woman from Hilo, who spoke nothing but English. All three nurses had been trained at the University of Hawaii. My respiratory therapist (again, a woman) was a Caucasian from Indiana; she had lived in Hawaii for fifteen years.

Interaction with local nurses began in much the same way as it did with flying nurses, but it progressed much faster in getting into biographical particulars. Both kinds of nurses would enter my room for the first time, introduce themselves, and say, "I hear you are a professor at UH." I would nod my head. The next question would be what department was I in. This was the first hurdle. The flying nurses would guess and would almost never get it right. And they would not usually use my alphabet board, even though it was lying next to my bed and they had been shown how it worked. The local nurses, though, would begin to use my board, perhaps because they had the knowledge and motivational culture to formulate themselves conversationally as members of the same social space. Hawaii has a strong culture of differentiating those who belong from those who are visitors or just passing through. Once my academic department had been identified, the local nurses would know where it was: "You are in Porteus Hall." Then would come statements like, "I took a sociology class from Ikeda" or "I studied biology with Sakumoto." I could then ask, "Who did you have for medical-surgical nursing?" We could progress quickly to a conversational exchange of personalities: "What did you think of X? How did you like the class? Where did you go to high school? Where did you grow up?" I could tell the local nurses I lived in Kailua and they would immediately ask me what neighborhood. They would know a lot about me from the neighborhood.

The local nurses had the conversational moves that indicated both a detailed knowledge of place and the motivation to use it as the basis of formulating co-membership in the social topography with me. This shared body of knowledge was identical with who (with substantial variation) we were. We, both myself and the local nurses, could be called out and motivated by these deep attachments.

Other Interactional Problems

I encountered a number of other routine difficulties with both flying and local nurses and with other direct care providers. I call the first two problems "Not Now" and "Out of Context." "Not Now" would occur either when I indicated I wanted to say something or when I was in the middle of formulating a sentence. I would be told "not now" as a way of breaking the interactional focus, rearranging the interaction to permit something else to happen. I would be interrupted from speaking when the crew of the portable X-ray machine crew would appear in my doorway, when my physicians or residents would enter the room, when any new machine would be set up, when my medications would be administered, and when I would be fed. Even when I was speaking about the procedure under way or about to begin, I would be cut off. Frequently, I was trying to tell personnel how to handle my body during the procedure. I had gained a lot of experience about what worked in the positioning of my body. Certain postures would cause coughing spasms and delay or abort the procedure. "Not Now" would happen every morning at seven when the X-ray crew would reposition me for a chest film and I was interrupted from telling them how to position me. Ignoring what I was trying to say, the crew would begin to move me and I would invariably go into a muscle and coughing spasm, ruining the X ray. I found little collective memory among X-ray crews, or among hospital staff, about what worked and what did not work, belying the fiction of nursing notes and staff conferences. I felt it necessary to direct each staff group away from problem areas in the handling of my body. But because I could not overlay my speech with ongoing action, and because paying attention to my speech required such a focus, I was usually unsuccessful in using my speech to guide the interaction.

"Not Now" is directly related to "Out of Context." "Not Now" can take three avenues. The first is simply saying the words when I am trying to speak. The second is when the party I am speaking to cuts me off by attending to another task, usually walking away in midsentence. The third avenue is when another person interrupts my conversation, taking over the interactional focus. "Not now" does not occur only when I am about to start a treatment or a procedure. It can happen anytime I am trying to speak.

"Out of Context" happens when I am able to resume speaking to the topic that I was addressing when I was interrupted with a "Not Now." Usually the interaction has moved along so far that when I address an old topic my conversants have a hard time grasping the relevance of what I am saying. It takes so much effort to spell out my words that I could not easily recycle the topic by saying, "You know what we were speaking about a little while ago, the X topic." I could only, because of time and energy, refer directly to a past topic. This speaking out of context would generate many complaints and much confusion. It would often break off further communication. Speaking out of context would be like an ethnomethodological experiment, producing comments such as "Are you crazy?" and "What the hell are you talking about?" The local nurses came to learn that this was a standing problem with my speech and would try to remember the course of our conversation. But it was often problematic whether they could remember, and it provided an opportunity for closing our talks, much to my frustration.

I found I could not do the constant reparative work that goes on in normal conversations. I did not have the temporal dimension to say "You know what we were talking about before" as a method of reintroducing a topic I had been discussing. I could not layer my speech with body gestures and with differentiations in pitch, volume, tone, stress, or pace of voice to keep my present turn at talk, keep from being cut off, and keep from having my sentences completed by others. Some persons would anticipate words as I was progressing through spelling them, unintentionally giving me words I had not thought of. The more common problem was and still is that other people finish my sentences, usually making me say something I had not intended. This has caused many sharp disagreements. Because I could not talk while my translator was reading what I said, I frequently experienced gross editing of my remarks. Sometimes the translator would refuse to say my thoughts. More frequently, she or he would not be assertive and translate them at the proper spot in the conversation, choosing to wait, delaying my participation and leading to still more out of context remarks.

Another trouble I had was that it was difficult to tell when my turn to talk was coming to an end, and, without the paralanguage of intonation, it was difficult to know when I had actually ended a turn. This was so harmful to the conversation that my conversant could not remember what I had just said. We had to start all over again, spelling out the sentence.

The last in this brief sample of interactional difficulties in the hospital is the absence of redundancy. Normal conversations are filled with countless restatements and qualifications of the topic and its predicates as the participants continuously negotiate and respecify meaning. My spelling out sentences was too labor intensive and focused to allow me to be sensitive to the need to rephrase and reinterpret my meaning in a given context. Tied down to looking at the spelling as it was written, I was usually unaware of behavioral signs of the need to respecify, and I was at a loss in formulating a proper interpretational context. Sometimes it seemed as if my statements came out of the blue, obscuring the interactional fit and meaning of what I said.

I started my paper with the intention of describing the ontological insecurity experienced in personal absorption into a complex of monitor screens in the ICU. I had been interested in the fragmentation of the post-modern personality.

When I began writing I entered the qualification that I cannot talk. I thought this colored my experience, making a difficult time even harder. However, when I began to think of how my body and my person were fragmented by the monitors, I could not get beyond the thought that there was a learning process in my looking at the nurses looking at the monitors and talking about what they saw. I was directed to look at and read the monitors from the attention given to them by these same nurses. It became a coordinated looking and reading. Because I was alone much of the time and could not ask questions about the monitors and what they meant by speaking, I tended to spend a lot of time looking at the screens and trying to figure out what they meant on my own. When I tried to communicate with the nurses I failed most of the time; 90 percent of them were flying nurses. I could not tag them with my face, gaze, or identity, thus pulling them into conversations.

As much as I was attracted to the notion of monitor screens, I came to doubt that they were the source of my trouble. Further, I came to see that postmodern social theory, at least as represented by Fredric Jameson and Jean Baudrillard, has no sense of social interaction (Tucker 1993). If the social is dead, as Baudrillard would have it, this common culture truth is an interactional achievement of talk, writing, film, broadcasting, drama, teaching, and other forms of discourse. The source of my difficulties in the ICU was in the daily social interaction with nurses, physicians, and technological people and in the meaning this interaction generated for the social and physical environment, including machines in the room. The absorption into monitor screens was produced, in large part, by my comparative isolation and inability to get information about the monitors and their read-out values.

I have described some of the communication problems I experienced in the ICU. I have come to see interaction, from its earliest phases of glancing and starting to talk, as the site of personal integration or fragmentation, security, power and powerlessness, anger, patience, memory, and context relevance in my attempts to talk in the hospital. The institutionalized, naturalized, socially consensual order of conversation has a rhythm, a time order, that assumes an intersubjective coordination of physical human bodies. Having a body that could not inhabit this time order breached the normalized conversational environment every time I tried to talk. Yet, as I learned from the local nurses, a few people demonstrate that the normal time order is but one among many time orders and structures for communication.

4 Anger

I am an expert on anger.* Not only can I assemble anger on a routine basis, I can see and talk about the sequential and socially concerted steps building toward an outburst before it happens. I am a virtual black belt in giving and receiving affronts to the assumption that we are in a common, intersubjective world (Schutz 1967). Over and through the course of interaction with me, as I try to effect normatively understood communicative moves, "interpretive asymmetries" (Coulter 1975) occur between me and my interlocutors. These asymmetries resemble, to a lesser extent, Melvin Pollner's (1987) "reality disjunctions" in formal dispute resolution settings such as courts, mental hospitals, or scientific debates (Goodwin 1994; Lynch 1993). My interpretive asymmetries grow subtly, as I usually fail to effect the talk and understandable body moves to create, sustain, and dissolve social engagements. Often, at least at first, my interlocutors do not notice an interpretive asymmetry. When they do notice they are frequently befuddled, since the source of the communication trouble is not obvious.

Often, those who communicate with me become impatient. I have to speak through a lip-reading translator, spelling out words letter by letter, frequently having to repeat forgotten or mistakenly heard letters. Some people

---

*I cannot stipulate what anger is. What is pleasing to some drives others up the wall. What is amusing in one context is maddening in another. My expertise is an extreme and "strong" example of Garfinkel's unique-adequacy requirement (Garfinkel and Wieder 1992).

complain they cannot find their own sense of interactional competence in my elongated replies, and they break off further interaction after voicing this grievance.

Then, too, when I do not have a lip-reading translator, my limited and weak body movements are often read as equivocal by my interlocutors, leading to repetition and frustration on my part and theirs. Also, I find myself estranged from a reciprocal competence in a common culture (Garfinkel 1967) when people speak slowly to me, over-enunciate, speak loudly, and tell me I have forgotten who they are when I full well remember them.

My expertise in anger does not lie in the disagreement sequences of normal conversational interaction. Of course I have these kinds of disagreements, as does every conversationalist. The situations I am writing about here are far more radical and disruptive to one's feelings of competence. I have experienced all kinds of interactive behavior that makes me think I am being treated as an incompetent interactant: (1) while I am working with my office computer, a caretaker will remove me from my office, suddenly and without notice, usually to take me home or to an appointment; (2) when I meet someone on a campus path and they indicate they want to talk to me, the caretaker who is pushing my wheelchair will not stop; (3) once engaged in interaction, I often experience myself being removed from the setting by a caretaker who is not following the interaction or who is following a separate timetable from the ongoing conversation; (4) frequently, caretakers will partially disrobe me, undertake medical procedures, or both in full public view; (5) when I am sitting in a comfortable position, a caretaker will decide I am not in the right posture, grab me, and jerk me into the caretaker's idea of how I should be sitting; and (6) often caretakers either will not consult me about transfers from my wheelchair to the office chair or to the car, or else they will take completely independent action, without informing me of what they are doing. Not only are these situations socially embarrassing, they can be dangerous. Being jerked into the 'right' postural position can tear my spastic muscles and result in joint pain. I am a big man and transfers take my cooperation, in the form of relaxing certain muscles and bearing weight. If I do not know what is going on in transfers, I cannot plan to relax my muscles or anticipate when I will bear weight. It is in these situations where the caretaker does not communicate about transfers that I am dropped, suffering multiple bruises and cuts. When I am not the one who decides what I will do and for how long, and when I am jerked around and sometimes fall, my anger quickly turns from disagreement to rage.

When I find myself being addressed by interactional practices that exclude me from a realm of interactional competence, and portend further exclusion, I usually protest vigorously, often with visible signs of anger. Because interaction is built sequentially, and the relevance of any practice of body or voice can be transformed by a subsequent move in the sequence, I can never be sure that any one utterance, positioning, or posture that appears exclusionary will imply further exclusionary behavior. However, I inhabit a biography where the first exclusionary practice, particularly by strangers, most often implies another. I am sometimes wrong about the order of implication of a first exclusionary practice, but not often. The estrangement from interactional competence continues until further notice or until proved wrong. Of course, if someone properly indicates an analysis of my communicative behavior, my own sense of competence is at stake; I am implored to indicate a proper analysis of their behavior.

But most times I take preemptive action, harshly responding to an exclusionary opening. By harsh, I mean my body becomes even more rigid than it already is, my facial muscles become spastic, I begin to shake, my veins stick out, my face becomes flushed, my eyes bulge, and I make every effort to look directly at my interlocutor. The response to my visible anger ranges from "I did not know you could hear," or "Oh, you can think!," or "Most of my patients are stroke victims and have trouble understanding me" to "Oh, I am sorry, I won't do it again." Most persons react to my outburst by ignoring me, which I take as a further documentary reading of my symptomatology by my interlocutor. It is a toss-up if my harsh reaction will change the course of interaction. Frequently those who say "I did not know you could . . .," or "I am sorry, I will not do it again" go back to exclusionary practices in a few moments.

The anger I am talking about is locally achieved, in and through the changing relevancies of ongoing interaction. It does not arise within a general social order, but within the social order achieved through *just* this talk and bodily behavior, with *just* these people or social members, and with *just* what these members make of the talk and bodies. What is extractable from this situated interactional order is provisional at best, a provisional inventory of how the perception of disabled bodies is itself an interactional category.

I not only receive exclusionary practices, I give them as well. People come to doubt their interactional competence when they interpret for me. When I am spelling out words letter by letter, forming my lips in barely perceptible signs for each alphabetic character, my interlocutors often become confused and frustrated; they look away, and even become humiliated to the point of real anger. Some words are real problems, necessitating repeated repairs. For example, a word that starts with T H has many lexicographic possibilities. My interlocutors often jump ahead of me when I have lip-spelled T H and fill in the missing letter as E, completing the word T H E. I often do not intend to use the word T H E—I might want to use THIS, THESE, THEIR, THEN, THAT, or THOROUGH or THREE or THROW. Such anticipation and false completion is a constant problem and requires many restarts in spelling the whole word. It is enough here to say that these difficulties often lead to stomping, pounding on desks and keyboards, and even to a refusal to interpret my lip signing. Not all persons lose their temper when interpreting my lips, but it has happened so often it has become an expectation.

In the remainder of this chapter I will describe and analyze two settings. Each involves anger or the portent of anger as experienced by me and my interlocutors. The first setting is a botched encounter in a shopping mall. The second is an outdoor party. I will then address the suggestion that I locate my anger in a universal, positive social space, such as the history, psychology, and anthropology of anger.

The Shopping Mall Encounter

One day an old friend, a former sailing buddy, approached me from behind and placed his hand on my back, saying, "I have not seen you in a long time." He continued, "I see your kids but not you." My friend is a pediatrician who has taken care of my four children. We met fifteen years ago when I spent a sabbatical year in the Department of Pediatrics at the University of Hawaii.

I wanted to speak to my friend. But he moved so quickly to my left side, while I was looking to the right to find a translator, that the eye and facial contact needed to initiate a conversation was barely apparent. He was soon up the adjacent stairway with his son, saying, "Er, it was nice seeing you." I was completely defeated in my attempt to meet with him. This entire encounter at the shopping mall was over in fifteen seconds. As soon as his hand was on my back, the first utterance made, the tonal quality immediately identifying my friend, I knew I was in trouble. I could not turn my head or swivel my body to respond facially to the greeting or opening statement and the hand on my left shoulder. I do not have the arm strength to move my wheelchair, and I am dependent on others to position it; likewise, I do not have the capacity to turn my sitting body. My friend moved from behind me to a nine o'clock position to my left. I glanced at him there for a moment and began to search for my wife on my right to translate for me. Unfortunately for the purpose of interaction, people push the wheelchair from behind, out of the range of vision and largely beyond the orbit where they can be cued that I want to speak to a passerby. I swung my head to the right and my neck and head dipped down to a forty-five degree angle; when I made eye contact with my wife she put a suction wand in my mouth and suctioned out the excess saliva. I could not even begin to start lip-signing letters to my friend through my wife. After his brief greeting, my friend bounded up the stairs and was gone before I could make the appropriate moves to start a conversation. I was seething with anger.

I want to say four things about this disastrous encounter. They are about face or gaze contact, time as a commonsense structure of interaction, the disinclination to interpret, and the tacit and interactionally implicative knowledge of seeing someone in a wheelchair, involved with his or her disability.

The first topic can be dispatched quickly. Mutual gaze is well documented as a practice for setting up, maintaining, regulating, and terminating face-to-face communication (Treichler et al. 1984). It is obvious that I sought and failed to establish mutual gaze with my friend, at least long enough for a mutually interpreted conversational opening.

Second, the time I want to address is not clock time but the intersubjective appreciation of looking at one another, looking away, looking at the interlocutor's other bodily involvements, and looking back at the face of the interlocutor. It is not objective time but the mutually interpreted coordination of gaze and other bodily movements; what the interlocutor makes of you, what you make of him, and what each makes of the interpretation of the other. This time is contingent time: what each makes of moves and utterances and countermoves and utterances, to see if one move is connected to another, the implicature between behaviors of interactants being continuously interpreted over the course of the interaction. My failure to sustain a reciprocal gaze, by looking at my friend, could have been overridden by my voice, if I had one. I might have said, "Wait a minute, I want to talk to you"; my wife could have said, "He wants to talk to you." However, there were no intervening verbal invitations to talk.

The third topic is the disinclination to interpret for me. Rendering my lip-signed letters into words can turn the interpreter into an interactional dope, a person who is demonstrably unsure of what he or she is saying, unendingly confused, someone without a memory, and the agent of one mistake after another. Being made to seem an interactional dope often leads to great outbursts of anger from my interpreter, including public denunciations directed at me. An inventory of problems in lip reading appears in Chapter 3; I will summarize them here. The following routine problems are associated with lip-reading my attempts to articulate individual letters: (1) many people cannot remember the preceding letters in a sequence and often substitute incorrect ones, resulting in having to respell the word; (2) even when they correctly remember the letters, some often cannot recognize the completed word, making it necessary to spell out the same word several times; (3) many cannot remember preceding words in the sentence, after correctly spelling and saying them, requiring me to respell the entire sentence; (4) many anticipate the letters of the words as I am spelling them, finishing the spelling for me. This is a big problem when the lip reader is wrong, which is most of the time, compelling me to start spelling over again; and (5) aside from completing my spelling, a few interpreters complete my sentences, even paragraphs. The result is often an incorrect statement of what I wanted to say, frequently giving it an unintended shading. In all cases, it robs me of the feeling that I am formulating my own thoughts.

Translating my thoughts to another person can make an idiot of the intermediary. Not all of them have the same trouble, and some can interpret for hours without major problems. I have the impression that for the few who regularly encounter every problem listed above I spell out words and make sentences too slowly for their spectrum of rhythms of hearing and assembling talk. Even though I ask these people to not finish spelling my words and completing my sentences, they appear to be unable to stop. I think it is their range of rhythms of hearing and speaking that is to blame. Their anticipation is just too strong.

Some people who regularly have the entire inventory of problems listed above stand out of the range of my gaze or on the borders of my gaze to escape my notice. With a history of interpretive problems, feeling very uncomfortable when they are pressed into acting as an intermediary, and not wanting to appear as interactional idiots, these people try to avoid the intermediary role. At some level they know that I know their bodily positioning, with their gaze directed away from me, signals their reluctance to serve as interpreters. When these people are the only ones around who I can turn to in an effort to communicate, their positional efforts to avoid the intermediary's role often anger me.

The fourth and last topic I want to consider in relation to the mall encounter is bodily engagement or involvement. I am seen as a person paralyzed, immobile to the interactional surround. The mere sight of me, as well as other disabled people I have observed in malls, often generates head shaking, scowls, even audible cursing. It is reputed this derision stems from fear, the "There go I but for the grace of God" syndrome. It is said that witnessing a disabled person is equivalent to seeing one's own mortality. I think these reasons have little to do with the derision. I surmise that in the perception of others one sees the full range of bodily instrumentalities and potential instrumentalities, calling out and institutionalizing, moment by moment, one's own bodily capacities and opportunities; the sight of the paralyzed, the crippled, the lame is a sharp denial of this commonsense, reciprocal knowledge. But this is a topic for another time.

The Party

The other setting I will use to explicate anger is a party after my son Thomas's soccer (football) game. It was the final match of the season, and the parents had brought food for an outdoor potluck lunch. They were arranged in an oval, with some of the children romping in the middle and some sitting with their parents. The food was on two picnic tables on one side of the oval. There were twelve sets of parents, along with some grandparents.

I was wheeled into the middle of the oval, facing the food tables. I was accompanied to the party by my wife and two people I will call X and Y. Divina left to talk to the coach and to make the rounds of the parents, most of whom we only vaguely knew. X and Y sat on a mat immediately behind me, completely out of my sight. Y can read my lips, X cannot. I quickly felt out of place in the middle. I could not see the few people I knew. Besides X and Y, these included only one other couple. They were sitting on a mat off to my right and behind me, and I could not easily exchange glances with them.

I came to see that a large part of socializing is accomplished in glance and facial gesture work. Looking at unknown others and looking then at friends, showing interest by looking at the same persons, and smiling and other facial gestures constitute mutual appreciation of the party setting. This visual activity produces much of the action at parties. I looked at grossly fat people, heard many jokes in Hawaiian pidgin, watched and heard the awards ceremony for the soccer players, saw kids play, and felt myself straining to look to my right where the couple I knew were sitting. I wanted to instinctively, perhaps, do the work of mutual gaze and facial gesture that would compose being in these visual scenes with others. I tried without success to engage X and Y to either serve as mutual appreciators or facilitate interaction with my friends.

My wife, standing on the outer edge of the oval, seeing me trying to turn my body to make eye contact with the people I knew, called out to X and Y to move where I could see them. They moved six inches, still out of my gaze. Divina came over to me and said, "I know you want to be involved, but you will have to wait."* I asked her to move me to be aligned with the people making the oval, but before I could finish my statement she was called by my son. She was off in a fraction of a second. I remained in the socially incongruous position near the middle of the oval.

I stayed there until I left the party. Finally, a conversational knot of people came near me. I could clearly hear them talking. Although no one addressed me or looked at me, I felt for the first time geared into the party. I followed the conversation, laughing at the funny points. A Portuguese-Hawaiian man was telling funny stories in Hawaiian pidgin. When Divina joined the knot, I felt I could look directly at the group members. My wife could deal with the contingencies of identifying me and translating for me if someone addressed me.

Just when I felt I belonged, though marginally, to the party, I felt myself being removed from the position where I was following the conversation. X, without warning, started to wheel me backward out of the party. I began to move my head and trunk in the most vigorous manner I could muster. X still continued to wheel me backward. I was confused, as no one had told me we were leaving and I saw no indication that the party was ending. I kept wriggling my body, and in a moment of absolute frustration I was able to remove my right foot from the wheelchair's foot rest and dig my toes into the ground. It was an effort to both protest my removal and retard my backward journey. The chair slowed but did not halt. I dug my toes harder into the grass. Still, I could not stop my removal.

---

*"Wait" is a word I constantly hear. The repetition of people telling me to wait has two meanings for me. The first is that I will not be part of the ongoing interaction. The second meaning has the echo of a complaint. The complaint is that my demand to be part of the interaction is a burden.

I was steaming mad. Y finally came around where I could see her and asked what was the matter. I spelled out, "T H I S I D I O T I S M O V I N G M E O U T O F T H E P A R T Y ." "Who is the idiot?" she asked. I indicated X by pointing my head. If I could have said idiot I would have uttered Idio—T! My anger was compounded by the long history of X placing my wheelchair in socially inappropriate positions, the refusal of X and Y to sit where I could see them in response to my wife's request, the avoidance of my gaze by Y in an effort to not serve as my interpreter, and the general frustration of twisting in the social wind of the party for so long. I was also mad at Divina for not facilitating my social interaction at the party.

At this point Y immediately began to strike her temples and breasts with her fists. She called me an ingrate and said, "X is only trying to help you; you just don't like him." I took her flagellation and utterances as indexical of three wider social texts. First, efforts in caring for disabled persons are not to be criticized. Any assistance should be accepted with a grateful smile. My criticisms of socially embarrassing care or care that is potentially or actually injurious has generated wounded comments from lay people and professional nurses: "Who is he to criticize?" "You have a nerve, criticizing me!" "You have no right!" "Who the hell do you think you are?!" "Do you have any idea of how hard it is to take care of you?" Y has said in the past, in the face of my criticism, "I try so hard to take care of you and this [your anger] is what I get." With regard to the second social text, I saw and heard the behavior of Y as epitomizing a long history of her response to any form of criticism of her or her husband, X, from anyone: she emotionally explodes, generalizing the specific criticism to any number of unrelated things. Of course I have to admit calling her husband an idiot is a global characterization that does not invite a specific response to a criticism. Third, and finally, I saw and heard her utterance about my not liking X as an example of her overgeneralizing a point of criticism, raising the level of conflict to unmanageable proportions, elevating the possibility of "If you don't like us we will leave you." At no point did Y address my observation and obvious criticism that X was moving me out of the party. My calling him an idiot may have made this impossible.

For Y to become angry with me increased my own anger in an ambivalent way. I was not as steaming angry with her as I was with X. I felt as if the situation were hopeless. I had seen this reaction from Y countless times before. No amount of explanation would work; Y was beyond listening to anyone. She kept hitting her breasts, and expressing every gesture and posture to indicate her anger had taken total possession of her.

To this day, I do not know if my withdrawal from the party was by verbal agreement or nonverbal communication between Divina and X and Y. What I do know is that no one communicated to me that we were leaving. Both X and Y were standing behind me when my wheelchair started to move backward. My wife was standing twenty feet away, talking to the soccer coach. If she had said something, I could not have heard her over the adjacent conversations. I did not see her speaking to me or to X and Y. My departure was a complete surprise. X never said a word, even through the histrionics of his wife. He kept moving my wheelchair until I was at my car. I am confused as to whether we left because we created an embarrassing scene as X moved me or because there was some prior communicated agreement that we were leaving.

The party was an exhibition of strived for and failed uses of the body and voice to create and maintain participation in a social event. The position of my wheelchair was wrong, and the range of my gaze was too restricted, to effect participation with others. I had no one to serve as a translator, and those who could serve avoided my gaze. I found myself constantly searching for the glance of those I knew; failing in that, I searched for the gaze of anyone. I was not successful. When I became a vicarious participant in a proximal conversational knot, following the topical and turn-taking structure, moving ever so slightly to the rhythm of the talk, I was abruptly removed from the party. Finally, my anger was amplified by my history with Divina and X and Y. I saw their avoidance behavior and emotional reaction to my anger as indexical expressions of that history.

Everyday Anger and Scholarly Treatments of Anger

I am aware that there are many ways to talk and write about anger. My ethnomethodological analysis of it, as well as my claim of unique adequacy in anger, is just one of the possible discourses. Even though I have argued that the anger talked about above is local to *just* that setting and *just* those people, I know anger has a history (see Stearns and Stearns 1986). The story of anger presented by Carol Stearns and Peter Stearns compellingly argues that it has been subject to a variety of positive and negative sanctions.

Not only does anger have a differential history, it also has a cultural anthropology (Epstein 1992; Levy 1973; Murphy 1987), a sociology (Kleinman and Copp 1993; Franks and Doyle McCarthy 1989), a psychology (Bertocci 1988), a psychotherapy (Hauck 1974), a medical analysis (Siegman and Smith 1994), and level upon level of lay understandings of those disciplinary analyses of anger. It is argued that the expression of anger and its recognition, as well as the reaction to it, vary by culture and by class status. Some cultures and classes permit and positively sanction anger: threats, verbal abuse, and public denunciations are readily taken to and are seen in a positive light, even glorified. Expressing anger, particularly of the self-righteous kind, can be viewed in many cultures as enhancing the person.

In psychology (Glick and Roose 1993), psychotherapy, and medicine, anger may be considered pathological. If it is repressed it has to be "let out," constructively "vented." There are angry families, socializing their members, generation after generation, as angry and violent personalities. Anger is pointed to as a causative or exacerbating factor in hypertension and cardiovascular disease. Additionally, there are normal life events, such as disablement (Gartner and Joe 1987), illness (Rosengren 1980), aging (Burke and Sherman 1993), and the death of loved ones (Kübler-Ross 1981), which are thought to generate anger. Although this anger is conceived as naturally generated, it still is theorized as something that must be dealt with and accommodated. Anger, in all its forms, both natural and pathological, is subject to intervention and management by the helping professions.

There are some management psychologists (*Industrial-Organizational Psychologist Newsletter*; Landy 1985) who try to rid the workplace of anger. Not only is "a happy work place more productive," but there is a discourse, endorsed by all, that an environment free of anger permits more-rational thinking. In 1994, Bob Woodward reported in *The Agenda* (Woodward 1994) that one of the criticisms of President Bill Clinton is that his temper gets in the way of formulating policy rationally.

Multiple discourses about anger litter the public consciousness. Some of the versions of anger derive from the professional and academic disciplines. Some stem from the common stock of lay knowledge. Most of them are overlapping and often mutually contradictory. Consider, for example these formulations: "Oh, he is an angry man!" "His anger is eating him." "You have to let your anger out." "They are angry people." "You have to control your anger." "His anger is destroying him." "You can't see straight because you are angry." "That must make you angry." "You only said that because you are angry." "You cannot think because you are angry." "He is motivated by anger." "His anger is out of control." "No one can get near him because he is so angry." "Such hostility!" "His anger will kill him." "You have to use your anger to do something creative." "Work off your anger!" "You should see someone about your anger." "You should see him when he's angry." "One of the most important things a parent can do is to teach children how to control their tempers." "His anger is destroying him and everyone around him." "You have to be angry to be a professional football player." "Angry parents, angry children." The list goes on and on. And the pronoun "she" can be substituted for the pronoun "he" in every such sentence.

I am a member of this array of commonsense lay knowledge about anger; I use it in interaction, thereby building social structure with my interactants. While I may smile now at the performative character of such statements as those listed above, in everyday interaction they are used in a concrete referential way, producing a mutual world of positive referents. Even though I may not agree with these statements, or the social structure they perpetuate, I am intractably drawn into using them—my person, perhaps my identity, is embedded in the exchange of statements in which I become a positive referent.

I am also a participant in the specialized discourses about anger. I can talk the history, anthropology, psychology, psychotherapy, sociology, and medical science of anger as a positive referent. The referential matrix of positive denotations to anger in this specialized, "scientific" knowledge builds up a positive social structure of use, including my utilization of the term and its referential object. In this way the knowledge assumes an objective, constant, constraining structure, which includes me as an actor within real circumstances.

Many persons have urged me to locate the anger described in the shopping mall and the outdoor party, in what amounts to the social space of these scientific knowledges of anger. I have not been eager to confound (Cicourel 1964) my topic, interactively generated anger, with an unanalyzed differential social setting or space, the specialized knowledge of anger.

Granted, the setting of my experienced anger and the specialized knowledge of anger are both interactionally produced. But to confound my experience of anger with the constructions of specialized knowledge is to miss the point of my analysis. I want to be very clear about what I am attempting: the descriptive analysis of how the body—voice and movement—is read as an ongoing, situated indication of normative knowledge in collaboratively constructed social settings. I am trying to describe (through what my neuromuscular incapacities make apparent) how the body brings off the intersubjectively recognizable activities of a successful meeting in the mall or the body movements and voicings that make up being at an outdoor party. My failed attempts to initiate and maintain eye contact and conversation, as well as my unavoidably less than successful reliance on others to position me and translate for me, can be considered ethnomethodological demonstrations of the embodied commonsense knowledge used to "do" a chance meeting in the mall and to "do" a party. My anger and frustration were generated by the refusal of my body, even with the assistance of others, to exhibit the textual signs of participating in those events.

If I were to locate the anger I have described in any one of the other disciplines—history, for example—it would be equivalent to giving up my analysis of how the situated body is used and read as the text of social structure. The use of history, as in saying my anger was typical of a historical epoch, would shift the focus of my analysis to something other than the bodily and interactionally contingent exhibition of commonsense texts to construct recognizable social settings. To impose a positive sense of history, irrespective of the interests of the bodies analyzed, negates the focus on situated bodily textual reading in interaction. This historical world—in the sense of a third party, positive history—is not one where actors exhibit bodily texts of common sense and then through the mutual reading and adjustment of those exhibitions jointly construct and dissolve social structures. Imposing a third-party, positive, universal history diminishes the actors to what Harold Garfinkel (1967) has called "judgmental dopes," people who do not know what they are doing.

5 Isolation

As my disease progressed I began to notice that I had become invisible to many friends and colleagues at the university where I am a professor. People with whom I had worked for many years and men and women with whom I had been friends for decades would pass by my wheelchair and not notice who I was. I would look them directly in the face, but they would quickly avert their eyes, gazing at a space about two feet above my head. People who knew me would pass my parked car, look directly at me, and show no sign of recognition.

A Columbia University anthropologist, the late Robert F. Murphy, first described this process of social isolation. Murphy had a spinal cord tumor and was eventually paralyzed at and below the level of the tumor. In his 1987 book, *The Body Silent,* Murphy details the dual process of the progression of his illness and the gradual loss of friends, colleagues, and visits by neighbors and family. As he lost physical functions, he increasingly found himself alone. I know Murphy's complaints well.

At home, I spend most of my time sitting in my lounge chair, reading or watching television. My father-in-law, who lives in the same house, has not addressed me in three years. My social life is limited to visits from relatives and to occasional parties we have at our house or at the beach. I do enjoy the company of my children, wife, and mother-in-law.

For reasons I still do not understand, students have been less put off by my condition than my colleagues and contemporaries. Throughout my illness I have maintained a stream of graduate students and research assistants. I have continued to teach, supervise theses and dissertations, and serve on a growing number of student committees.

I do not want to imply or say that I have been deserted by all my friends and colleagues. In fact, a few friendships have become stronger during my illness. These few have offered and have delivered every kind of assistance to me and my wife, Divina. Additionally, I have maintained contact with social science colleagues on the mainland and in Canada, Europe, the Pacific Islands, and Asia through regular mail, telephone, and e-mail.

The problem, as I see it, is one of distancing from local colleagues and friends. Although I have experienced universal support from my department, college, and university colleagues, making it possible for me to continue working, I rarely *see* these people. I also receive praise from old friends, suggesting that I have uncommon courage, but I do not often *see* these people, either. The texture and identity generated by daily face-to-face interaction with colleagues and friends has been absent from my life for years.

The Problem

My experience, the experience of Robert Murphy, and the experience of Kay Toombs (1992), an academic philosopher with multiple sclerosis, are recognizable stories. Erving Goffman, in his 1963 book, *Stigma,* gives many other recognizable examples of the social discrediting of those who suffer from visible disabilities and deformities. By "recognizable" I mean that the reader can analyze the stories to an infinite depth: they can be read as a signification of general knowledge (what anybody knows), of how "normal" people react to visibly disabled individuals; they can be read as a record of people who have withdrawn themselves from those who have become disabled, frail, or elderly; they can be read as a personal history of reaction to the visibly disabled; they can be read as a moral indictment of those who leave the disabled to their own devices; and they can be read as stories of personal tragedy and a plea for help by the disabled. They can be approached, as well, as an account of disabled people who have withdrawn themselves from the ordinary round of life.

Murphy's is a personal story of perseverance in the face of tragedy. Toombs's account concerns the eidetic, constant mechanisms of the body in constituting the world. The process by which texts reference specific bodies, movements, settings, characters, and documentary methods of common interpretation, thereby producing an experience of isolation or social abandonment, is entirely absent in Murphy, Toombs, and Goffman.

What is needed is a description of the ongoing, contingent, interactional production of experienced isolation. It is precisely the situated, temporally unfolding, interactional interpretation of isolation that is our topic. The specific acts of body and voice, and their reading, bring on this felt isolation.

Specific social relationships or practices produce an immediately felt isolation, along with other sources of estrangement, such as the time requirements of my medical care. What follows is a chronology of my typical day. The description focuses on specific interactional configurations (such as my bodily failure to enact the appropriate opening to conversations on the path to my building) and on a more general depiction of my daily routines.

Morning

When I awaken, around seven or eight, I begin watching CNN. This network is the background noise in life for myself and my wife. We watch it when we get up and when we go to bed. We know the announcers and reporters on both the international and domestic services. They are like familiar family members.

At eight-thirty, after Divina eats breakfast, we start with the first breathing treatment of the day. I am on a ventilator, which pumps a medical mist into my lungs to loosen the mucus. After the breathing treatment, I am turned on my left side, while my wife uses a percussor to loosen the mucus from my right lung. Then I turn on my right side and the percussor is used on my left ribcage. After this physical therapy of my chest is completed, the head of the automatic hospital bed is raised and I am thoroughly suctioned. Then Divina shaves me. I am amazed that she gives me a better shave than I ever gave myself.

After the shave, I get a bed bath. Then I am fed. By this time *Talk Back Live* is playing on CNN. (When it is three in the afternoon in Atlanta, it is only nine in the morning in Hawaii.) After I am fed, my wife cleans my trache. Then she will do range-of-motion exercises on my arms and legs. Then I will use the toilet.

This routine of care takes about three hours. We can plan no morning activities. (If we have an early morning date, like my son's soccer game, we have to get up at 5:00 A.M.)

We leave the house around eleven-thirty and arrive at the office at noon.

Scheduling

Isolation is not a constant, even though it may retrospectively be accounted for that way. It is best thought of as an interactional achievement, subject to all the contingencies and variabilities of situated interpretation.

Scheduling is a problem for the paralyzed. By "scheduling" I mean the ability or nonability to move your body and voice to demonstrate to your interactants that your behavior is responsive and conditioned by the behavior of others. William Condon (1974, 1976) and Eveoleen Rexford, Louis Sander, Theodore Shapiro (1976) have demonstrated the rhythms in adult interaction and those in adult-infant caretaking. Sander has also isolated certain postural forms of interaction; the forms communicate, often subliminally, the content of a major part of the interaction. Adam Kendon (1981) has a body of work on shared rhythms across communicants and an inventory of body language forms, both of which signal the construction of a specific kind of interactional engagement. Martha Davis (1982) has edited a book on interactional rhythms.

There is a basic difference in what I take to be the constructive-analytic, extractive interest in rhythms and coded body language of Sander, Condon, Kendon, and Davis and my own interest in the situational and contingent reading of body movement. I think Sander and others interested in rhythms and body language are trying to extract configurations of rhythms and recognized postural forms as objective, general constructions of interaction. I submit that configurations of rhythms and body language do not have contextless, general meaning. Rather, the meaning of shared rhythms, or asynchronous behavior and body codes, derive their specific meaning contingently in and through the course of interaction. The meaning is subject to change as the interaction develops and even after the interaction has ended, through the course of reflection.

I purposely use the term "scheduling," rather than "rhythms," to avoid the sense of constructionism and to refocus us on how members are constantly fitting rules, or background expectations, to the ongoing history of interaction.

Interacting from a Wheelchair on Campus

When I come to work, I transfer from my car to a wheelchair. My wife, or sometimes a friend, drives. The car is parked near my building and I have occasion to pass many friends, colleagues, and students on the way to the elevator. Because I am paralyzed and cannot talk, I have special problems hailing people and engaging them in conversation. The same problems come up when I make one of my rare voyages about campus or one of my frequent visits to shopping areas, malls, or the beach.

Three people are involved when I want to talk to someone. First, there is the person pushing my wheelchair. Second, there is the party or parties I want to interact with. Third, there is myself, sitting in a wheelchair, motionless except for limited head movement. A host of obstacles arise when I or others want to talk. The problems have a history, such that people learn of interactional difficulties firsthand or by report and avoid me when I am about campus. People have told me this, and I read their avoidance behavior accordingly.

There appear to be tactical problems in wheelchair pushing that make the pusher insensitive to interactional cues. The first is terrain. I am a big man, and it is difficult to stop the wheelchair on inclines to permit me to talk with people. My university building is on a slope, so many potential encounters in the vicinity are aborted by this difficulty. I now realize the importance of the flexible ankle, which permits maintaining balance on inclines while interacting face to face. The wheelchair is no substitute for the ankle.

A second problem leading to interactional insensitivity is that pushing takes a great deal of concentration, similar to driving a car. But, unlike a car, the wheelchair must share the walkways with pedestrians moving and standing at every angle. The pusher has to monitor the surface for holes, any unevenness that can catch the front wheels, and the sides of the walkway as well, lest the wheelchair go off track and turn over. The pusher has, also, to monitor the position of the foot rests, which extend in front of the chair and often out of his or her sight. I have had my wheelchair turn over on top of me, and I have had it run off curbs, severely injuring my side and feet. If the pusher is not aware of these possibilities, I make them known. The problem for me, amidst all the surface monitoring, is how to signal the pusher, the intended subject of conversation, successfully. I am sitting in a moving chair without the power of verbal salutation, without the power of gestural salutation, and with limited power of gaze salutation because of weak neck muscles. At best my postural and gaze salutatory efforts are ambiguous. It is difficult for the pusher or other intended subject of conversation to see in my behavior a recognizable request for talk. Usually the intended subject will walk by smiling directly at me, making some utterance of recognition to the pusher.

Another way of stating the problem is that the three parties—the pusher, myself, and the intended subject—must execute and recognize, and therefore schedule, the mutually interpretive signs that a conversation is desired. Some persons can read my ambiguous signs of salutation and request for conversation. These may be student-workers who can lip-read and can comprehend changes in posture and gaze, or they may be family members. If I do not have a trained student assistant or a family member around, what normally happens is that third parties standing in front of me, and therefore able to read my face and gaze, will signal my intended subject for conversation and the pusher that I want to talk. Usually, the pusher, standing behind me and focused on the contingencies of pushing a wheelchair with a high center of gravity, is the last one to know I want to talk.

There are what I call accumulated histories, read by me when I experience avoidance behavior by others. What I mean by "accumulated histories" is that when I see someone avoid me I see a whole historical deposit of embarrassments in having tried in the past to speak to me while I am in transit in my wheelchair. I see averted faces and the manifestation of overriding interactional involvements (as when friends pass in conversation and ignore me) as the sedimentation of past incidents of failing to get the attention of either me or the person pushing my wheelchair or, once stopped and focused on having the conversation, as the sedimentation of problems in translating my lip movements or of mutual embarrassment caused by my drooling and the need to have my mouth suctioned every minute. These accumulated histories are read into avoidance behavior en route from my car to my building on campus and in my journeys in the building's halls and around the walkways of the university. The sudden changes in direction by colleagues on foot, the avoidance of mutual gaze, the intense involvement in discussion or in contemplation of a noticeably deep muse, and a broad variety of other behaviors that can be assembled under the label of avoidance are often, but not always, read by this historical text.

I have talked of avoidance behaviors as I have witnessed them on the way from the car to my academic office building, have described some of the physical contingencies of being pushed in a wheelchair, and have laid out the historical text by which I frequently read the behavior of friends and colleagues. I experience these behaviors and their interpretations as repetitive, abiding, objective structures, even though I know the objectiveness is contingent.

The contingent character of these behaviors–interpretational structures is that they are repetitive and objective until proved otherwise. The validity of these interpretations, and therefore their institutional quality, is interactionally achieved. There are occasions in which my interpretations are subsequently proved wrong. There are times when persons (students, colleagues, friends) who have ritualistically avoided me suddenly break with the accumulated history and successively engage in every opportunity to interact with me. I have come to learn through my physical condition that part of interactional competence, for anyone, is exhibiting body moves and speech sensitive to interactional cues that do not meet the expectations of objective institutions. Such competence is the analysis and understanding of what is going on, both for the self and for exhibition to others.

The institutional nature of these behaviors-interpretations is only more or less. It is the experience of the repetitive, abiding avoidance that gives an institutional character to such avoidance. There is no comparative analysis of the frequency of avoidance behaviors and positive interactional initiatives.

The concrete validity of these behaviors-interpretations, their independence and generality as truth statements, resides in the personal experience of their being more or less true.

After many years of difficulties in hailing interlocutors on the pathways between the parking lot and my building and on rare longer trips around campus, Divina and I have devised a strategy for postponing the conversation. My wife, who is usually the pusher, will ask the interlocutor to come to the office to talk. I can better communicate there, with my lip-reading student assistants. Unfortunately, most of those who run into me on the pathways and are invited to the office do not come.

In the Office

Once I get to the office, via the parking lot and pathways, I begin work. I arrive at the office at noon. I transfer immediately to my office chair. I will sit in this comfortable chair for five or six hours.

The first thing I turn my attention to is e-mail. As the years go on, I find it to be one of my chief ways of communicating with colleagues at the University of Hawaii, even though they may be down the hall. I also use e-mail to stay in touch with friends and colleagues all over the world, exchange papers and grant letters, communicate criticism of papers and proposals to students, and correspond with my two older children.

I am consumed by e-mail for many reasons. I enjoy reading computer magazines, especially articles on e-mail and the World Wide Web. I find the technology involved and the rapid pace of its improvement amazing. But I am mostly immersed in e-mail because it is a chief source of interactional competence. I do not have the daily round of chats that I used to have before I became ill. My relative immobility makes it impossible to hop from office to office, meet people in the halls, cross paths with people in going from building to building, attend the number of meetings that I once did, and go to lunches, dinners, and parties. E-mail is how I get news of colleagues, friends, and relatives. Being up-to-date on what people are doing is important, as it establishes my currency on what is conversationally relevant and establishes, as well, my reflexive sense of personal competence in communication. I play back my current talk-about-ables across my selected e-mail recipients. For example, when a female friend e-mailed me about her divorce and remarriage, I was able, using my computer, to mention to a mutual friend that I had received a message from our friend about her situation; the mutual friend was able to e-mail me back with an elaboration of her remarriage to a man we both knew. In another application, colleagues in my college e-mail me their views on students' papers, proposals, and progress.

Exchanges on current topics with colleagues, friends, and relatives positions me as a person "who knows what is going on." It is as if talk-about-ables are dated in quality and cannot be as easily used after they are too old. They become old news or else retellings. Moreover, the information I get via computer is qualitatively different than the stories one gets from newspapers, news magazines, and television news. The stories received via e-mail are about people I know; the replay of the particulars in the stories to the friends who tell them and to others constitutes the material practice of keeping abreast with those friends and others. The currency of the stories positions me as a participant in what is happening now. My e-mail correspondence, at least my reading of it, permits others to say, "He knows everything."

Afternoon Work

After I dispense with my e-mail, which I will nonetheless revisit many times, I shift my attention to writing papers, meeting with students, working on my classes, or attending meetings. I like to think I devote most of my time to writing. But I can write without interruption only during the summer. I still come to the office, as I can only concentrate there.

During the regular semester, I am constantly interrupted while I am writing academic papers or chapters of books. Students drop by and want to talk or explain why they need my signature. I have developed an amazing ability to return to the spot where I was working before the interruption. I am surprised by this new ability. I did not have it before my illness and could and did get sidetracked by discussions with students, usually for the whole afternoon. My student assistants will often remark "We are going back to work now" when a student is half out the door. I am no longer irritated by such interruptions, treating them as times to let my mind subconsciously work on problems I could not solve straightaway.

I will spend the major portion of the afternoon working on my papers or talking with students. I will leave the office around six in the evening. However, I do not feel I spent my time well if I was not writing a paper. Too much time is spent with filling out administrative forms. Luckily, I usually get some writing time, even on the worst days.

I have few faculty office visitors. Those who do come leave shortly. Most ask me to do something, quickly tell me they are late for a meeting, and rush out the door. Only one fellow will sit and shmooze with me. He is Jon Okamura. We met in Manila, while I was a Fulbright Professor. We love to talk about the Philippines, Filipinas, and women in general. I also talk with Charon Pierson, an older graduate student who is also on the faculty of nursing. She is the first real ethnomethodology graduate student I have had. She has a deep commitment to the discipline, and I often think her ethnomethodological vision goes further than mine.

I talk a lot with my research assistants. We discuss my work, movies, and restaurants, and my students and my seminars. But mostly we focus on their career plans. For example, I am worried about one of my students finding what truly interests him in his Ph.D. program. I have repeatedly asked him to tell me one subject area that fascinates him. Another student needs help in being more sure of herself about what she has to offer potential employers. I tell her she has many talents and should be more sure of herself. A third assistant is wavering between going to medical school or veterinary school. We talk about her motivations for each. A fourth student wants to be a professor in a university. We talk about how to get a professorial appointment. I am very lucky to have had a long history of talented research assistants. I have no hesitations about counseling them or recommending them to employers.

Evenings

Around six o'clock Divina and I leave the office and go to the car. Transferring me is not an easy task. I have to be wheeled beside the front passenger door. My wife, in a demonstration of Herculean strength, stands me on my feet and turns me into a position where I can drop down to the seat. Once I am inside, she has to pull my legs into the car and then has to position me in the seat by grasping me by my armpits from behind and pulling up while I push with my legs. Then Divina puts my wheelchair in the back of our station wagon. Having accomplished this monumental task, we embark on the half-hour drive to our home in the suburbs of Honolulu.

When we get home, my wife and either my mother-in-law or father-in-law help me transfer out of the car to my home wheelchair. I then move to my easy chair in the family room, where I will remain till midnight. I read for about two hours in the chair, while *The Newshour with Jim Lehrer* plays in the background on television. I have a beeper, which I operate by turning my head, that signals my children to turn pages. Occasionally my son, Thomas, will ask if he can watch a program. I always assent. I enjoy his company.

After Divina has positioned me in the easy chair and suctioned me, she eats dinner and prepares dinner for the children. Around 7:30 Divina will go over Thomas's homework. At 8:30 she will go to bed for a nap. She will wake up at 10:45 and come into the family room, where I am watching TV, and sleep on the couch until 11:30. Around 11:45 she will begin to transfer me to bed. We will go to sleep around one in the morning, after a breathing treatment, chest physical therapy, trache care, feeding, and a light bed bath.

Weekends and Holidays

This evening routine is extended during the weekends. Then, I will arrive in the family room around noon and will read and watch television until midnight. I usually rent movies for Saturday and Sunday nights; the TV offerings are particularly awful on weekends. Half the time Divina will watch the movies with me. Sometimes Thomas will watch too, especially if it is an action movie.

I like to go to the beach. I used to sail a Hobie-Cat, and I enjoy watching the water, the ground swells, the wind action on the water, catamarans, wind surfers, fishing boats, and beach goers. We often park near the boat-launching ramp on Kailua Beach and watch the boat action. The ramp is next to the best beach on Oahu, the island where we live. Frequently my son will come along and go swimming in the aquamarine waters of Kailua Bay. Much to my regret we do not go to the beach often, now. The scene is enjoyable in itself, and it is one of the few places where my wife and I can talk.

One of my joys is watching Thomas play soccer on Saturdays. He is in an American Youth Soccer Organization league. He usually starts play at the end of August and finishes in December. He has been chosen for an all-star team, which plays from January until April. The games get me out of the house, and they provide a break from the mindlessness of television. Plus, I genuinely enjoy watching soccer, and my son.

I have a great deal of difficulty with three-day weekends. I find I cannot take the boredom that sets in on Sunday afternoon and intensifies on a Monday holiday. I feel as if the action for me, as a scholar, is when I am working. Extended holidays are a time out of productivity. There must be a pinch of Protestant ethic there. My wife enjoys staying home much more than I do.

Since my discharge from the hospital in 1991 after a serious case of pneumonia we have not received one invitation to go to dinner or to a party at our friends' houses. As of 1997, we have had a complete drought of invitations. Many have said, "We will have to have you over." But the actual invitation never comes. Now, Divina and I regard such statements as patronizing.

We have annual picnics at a local beach park. Along with my research assistants, we invite graduate students, faculty, and friends to a potluck picnic at Magic Island in Ala Moana Beach Park. These gatherings last four or five hours. They are a delight. It is one of the few times I can socialize as I did before my illness. One or more of my research assistants serves as a lip-reading translator while I engage in conversations.

My wife and I rarely invite people over for dinner at the house. During Christmas we may play host to what are known in Hawaii as calabash relatives (relatives by affiliation). We often talk about inviting others, but our sit-down dinners are infrequent. Although Divina is a truly good cook, she does not cook often; she seems consumed and exhausted by the effort. Although she thinks she has to cook original meals for guests, I am perfectly comfortable with delivered pizza or Chinese food. Having meals brought to our house would, I think, avoid the tension connected with cooking and make it easier to invite people over.

We do socialize with my research assistants. We go to restaurants with them. Paying for the meal is one way of thanking them for the excellent work they do for me and Divina and for taking such good care of me. I could not accomplish a thing without them. We used to have frequent potluck lunches in the office, and there is still a constant chatter about food there.

Their Backs to Me

Body behavior can be another form of unintended cut. Like the dissociation of intent from talk, as in the statement "It is only talk," body behavior exists on a level that can easily be repudiated. People routinely deny any intention behind gasps, sighs, grunts, audible inhalations or exhalations, playing with their hair, glasses, or fingers, closing their eyes for an extended period, rubbing the nose or face, or turning sideways or away from someone.

However, bodily behavior exists, and it has a commonsense reading. There is a consensus on what certain gestures mean, such as the audible sigh or "tsk" immediately following a request, which indicates resistance. The sigh or "tsk" constitutes a form of resentment at the request or against the requester. Yet, when challenged to explain what they mean, they usually deny that they sighed or tsked and they did not mean anything by whatever sound they made.

I want to talk about another form of bodily behavior. Like sighing or "tsking," it is easily disassociated from any intention. This separation is part of the commonsense culture of the behavior. What I am talking about is a redundant phenomenon. It is occasioned during visits to our house and sometimes during visits to my office. It has often happened during parties at the house. Over the course of conversation and general interaction people will often turn their backs to me, blocking my frontal access to the ongoing conversation. Sometimes this happens immediately after someone is introduced to me; he or she then quickly turns to another in the room and begins to talk. At parties I will frequently face a wall of the backs of people gathered in a conversational knot. The frequency of this phenomenon makes me think there is something about my personal appearance, movements, or my public designation as a disabled man that routinely leads people to avoid or ignore me. I often find myself inspecting my appearance for the stigmata of disability that would lead someone to exclude me from interaction.

I bear one of my biggest stigmata when I am at home: Divina puts a bib on my chest to catch the drool. I call it an idiot bib. Wearing a bib and drooling in it lets others categorize me as a stroke or a brain injury patient, quietly leading a vegetative life. (This is nothing but a cultural category, and I neither wish nor mean to impose it on stroke and brain injury patients.) But when people see me following a conversation with my facial gestures and then speaking through my wife they will often remark, "I did not know he could hear or speak." The wearing of the idiot bib leads to deductions that I am incontinent, deaf, and otherwise socially incompetent. When we have visitors, I ask Divina to remove it. Often, for one reason or another, the bib stays on. This almost always has the effect of socially stigmatizing me.

Another social stigma is the half-full urinal, left in full view of visitors. There is a similar set of deductions here about the control of bodily fluids, this time urine. The visible absence of fluid control leads to the same set of conclusions about being a stroke or a brain injury patient, or about being mentally retarded. In either case, the urinal with its yellow contents is a sign of social disqualification. When I have the slightest anticipation of visitors, I will ask and then demand that it be removed from sight.

The last incident I will mention is how the presence of a nurse set up a wall of bodily aversion and kept me out of the social interaction at my own birthday party. I will never forget driving up to our house, after doing chores, and finding a nurse standing by his car. The male nurse had taken care of me about ten times before. He was a good nurse and a good person. But I was shocked that I had not been informed he was coming to take care of me during my party. I vigorously protested what I considered a fundamental breach of communication.

I entered my house and sat in my easy chair, awaiting my guests. The nurse stood beside my chair; he was an off-duty army nurse and had the special characteristic of standing during his entire shift. Out of hundreds of nurses who have come to my house, this was the only one who refused to sit down, even when asked. The guests trickled in and had to pass in front of the standing nurse, who was positioned to my left, between me and the open room. He served as an unintentional buffer between me and the open room, where the guests had gathered. This physical barrier was made worse by the fact that the nurse could not lip-read and assist me in communicating with the few friends who made the effort to come in front and across him.

I was practically isolated in my own birthday party. I had few candidate interlocutors, and the few I had I could not communicate with. I was extremely angry and frustrated. Had I known a nurse was coming, I would have asked one of my student research assistants to be at the house when the party began. The student assistant would have helped me communicate. As it turned out, I was sitting in my chair, the nurse standing between me and the guests, and the guests gradually formed a conversational knot, with the majority turning their backs to me. I could not even hear what they were talking about. This lasted for almost two hours.

I was saved from total isolation when a student research assistant arrived. I was very lucky that Zhuo Miao was one of the fastest lip readers, with great word anticipation and context reading, almost bordering on mind reading. She sat on a stool near my chair and served as my communications intermediary. When she left after an hour and a half the situation returned to the structure of isolation, until my wife noticed the bad time I was having and came over to serve as my translator. This party has remained a sore spot with me, so much so that I have refused any further birthday parties.

Alone in the Company of Others

The experience of isolation is not static or constant, although it can on occasion be assembled that way. It is punctuated by distractions and interruptions, and it is continuously subject to the ongoing and contingent behavior of others. People in my surround are always moving and directing glances, and often talking; these behaviors are read by me, and I assume by others, as disclosing meaning and motivation. My sense of isolation is specific to my reading of behavior; it is also subject to the next set of behaviors, which may render my feeling of isolation irrelevant or retrospectively wrong.

The first setting is a bookstore with a coffee bar. The bookstore, Borders, is in the very popular Waikele shopping center, and it is usually jammed. We frequently go there and always patronize Borders, if only for getting slices of cake, apple tarts, and cups of cocoa in the coffee bar. Although the bookstore is relatively large, the floor space is constricted by bookshelves and magazine racks, leaving barely enough space for my wheelchair.

The section of the store where food is served is marked off by a long bar, running the length of the area of tables and chairs, making a right angle, extending about six feet, and setting off the entrance. There are three rows of tables and chairs; in addition, there are high stools along the bar, affording customers a flat area to eat, drink, and read. The entire coffee bar is congested, full of furniture, people, food, and reading material.

When my family wants to eat at the coffee bar, I cannot fit my wheelchair inside (It is rather large, commensurate with my tall body.) I am usually positioned on the outside of the bar, midway along its length, in the aisle between the bar and the book racks. Divina, who usually pushes my wheelchair in the bookstore, looks for an empty stool or two at the bar, anticipating that after she buys the pastries she can sit across from my position on the outside of the bar.

While my wife and family are standing in line at the coffee bar, I am left by the vacant stools. Occasionally people will approach the empty stools and ask me if this area is occupied. In reply, I will try to shake my head up and down to indicate yes. My neck is weak and I have trouble signifying an unequivocal yes. Sometimes my questioner can see I am affirming that the area is indeed occupied. He or she then leaves. At other times the questioner cannot read my affirmative answer, repeats or rephrases the question, and frequently, in the face of what seems equivocal body language from me, takes his or her seat on the empty stool.

A number of times parties, usually couples, will approach the vacant stools, hesitate, gaze at me directly or indirectly, and turn and walk away, only to come back in a moment and repeat the whole cycle of visibly assessing where they are going to sit. These parties do not ask me if this place is taken. They appear to scan the vacant area, look at me sitting across from it, partially turn to look for alternative seats in the coffee area, and then walk away.

If a couple actually sit on the vacant stools, they frequently turn their backs to me, occasionally facing the bar to sip their drinks or take a bite of cake. With their backs to me, they appear to be scanning the other people in the coffee area. Sometimes, I hear a couple discussing the people in view or the quality of the food or coffee. I am very close and can hear what they say, even at low tones.

Before I begin to analyze the isolation experienced at the bookstore, I want to remark on the same kind of isolation at my birthday party. Unbeknownst to me, my wife had arranged for a nurse to care for me during the party. Arranging nurses to care for me without consulting me or, at the very least, informing me before the nurse arrives has been a point of contention between me and my wife. Part of my objection to having a nurse on the occasion of the party and in similar settings is that by having a nurse standing by me, caring for me, a person who cannot read my lips, I feel separated from the people in my immediate surround. The nurse is a buffer, which most people will not penetrate. I find on social occasions that having a nurse is equivalent to being assigned the role of a permanent side participant, an overhearer, and an uninvolved visual witness. I am not an axial participant in face-to-face interaction when a nurse is caring for me.

Given the nurse on my birthday, the isolating event I will describe occurred when a married couple came over to my chair and the wife began to ask me a series of questions about my eldest daughter. "Is Adrienne coming this summer?" she asked. "Where is she now?" "Where is Terry?" "Is he coming?" "When are they coming?" To the questions about whether they were coming to Hawaii, I thought I had successfully nodded an affirmative answer. When I was asked when they were coming, I looked around for someone who could read my lips. Finding no one, I was left with the hope my interlocutor would ask me the month, so I could either nod my head yes or shake it for no. I was not to be so lucky. The wife repeated the question, "When are they coming?" And then she asked, "Are they coming?" Apparently my nodding at the first question when it was asked once and then again was seen as unresponsive. Immediately after asking "Are they coming?" and while I was nodding, she turned to her husband and said, "He doesn't know if they are coming or when they are coming." Her husband responded, "He must know." She replied, "I asked him and he doesn't know."

I knew my children were coming and I knew when they were coming. Obviously my nodding did not work. This was not the only time my nodding was seen as equivocal, as my troubles in the bookstore attest. Often people will ask of my lip-reading interpreter, "How does he say yes or no?" They register surprise when the interpreter mimics my nodding for affirmation and my shaking my head from side to side. "Oh," they say, "I should have recognized that." I take it the surprise is that they now see I was gesturing yes and no to their questions all the time. But except for the few students who work with me daily, the recognition that I was giving unequivocal answers all along is of little benefit in subsequent interaction. It is frequently evident that my nodding yes and head shaking no have not been seen as replies to conversational questions, even after my questioners have had a demonstration of the two sorts of gestures. I have no redundancy capability allowing me to utter "Yes, yes" or "Em, em" or "No, no" or "Nah, nah" in synchrony with my head nodding or head shaking. I have observed that most head indications of yes or no are accompanied by a contemporaneous verbalization of yes or no.

The feeling of isolation in the bookstore and in the encounter with the couple at the party does not essentially reside in the few minutes of being alone while waiting for my family to rejoin me or in being alone at a social gathering. The essence of isolation, at least for me, resides in the inability to indicate through my own bodily behavior and speech the analysis of others' preceding and subsequent utterances and bodily behavior. Both in the negotiation of reserving the space and stools at the coffee bar and in answering the questions about if and when my children were coming to Hawaii, my interlocutors could not tie their questions to my responsive behavior; in fact, they may not have been able to see any understandable response to their inquiries. The ability to indicate an analysis of preceding or contemporaneous actions by behaviors and utterances seen as connected to those preceding or contemporaneous actions is the foundation of mutually understood, coordinated interaction. These analytic demonstrations compose our everyday existence with others.*

The incapacity to witness an effect on the behavior of others is the estrangement called social isolation. Estrangement from indications of reciprocally witnessed analysis of behavior is not the same as stating that the estrangement is continuous or permanent. Estrangement is contingent on the relative absence of reciprocal analysis. There is always some degree of reciprocal analysis in gaze-to-gaze behavior, as in the fact that mutual gaze is taken by most to signify shared attention. Even though there is always some degree of common analysis of body positions, for the most part, when I have no one to translate for me, I find it impossible to affect the behavior of others. But there is always the possibility, infrequently realized, that someone will come up with a way of interacting to which my personal sense of competence will compel me to respond.

---

*I have the idea that analytic indications apply not only to behavior with others (such that a first greeting of "Hi" is answered and is seen to be answered by anyone by a second "Hi") but also to our relations with the extrahuman surround. Our interaction with nature and our movements have, more or less, a directed analytic character. Consider our gait: we move one foot in front of the other, in a tacitly conscious pattern of complicated muscle movements, simplified here as stepping off on the toes of one foot and landing on the heel of the other foot. Each muscle movement or muscle group movement demonstrates an analysis of the preceding and subsequent movements, as well as the individual's lived history of similar movements.

Traveling

Since my hospitalization six years ago, we have not traveled. This was a big lifestyle change for me and for Divina. We used to go places all the time, across the Pacific and to the U.S. mainland. Deciding to stay home had a negative impact on my two older children, who live in California. There are two reasons we stopped traveling. Because I am disabled, I need the assistance of two persons to make transfers and to help my wife with the many details of moving my equipment. Divina and I have not been able to save any money since my stay in the hospital, and the unreimbursed portion of the hospitalization costs almost wiped us out financially. We have not had the money to afford to travel with someone to help in transfers and to help with the equipment.

The second reason is that my medical condition makes traveling risky. During my hospitalization I had a trache installed. This is how I breathe. I have a constant leakage of excess saliva down my windpipe to my lungs. The saliva has to be suctioned out. Frequently, when the saliva builds up, or when I get a lung infection, I have shortness of breath. There is an additional concern about my getting enough oxygen in a pressurized airplane cabin at thirty thousand feet. My physician is not enthusiastic about my going on planes.

Telephone

Making calls is problematic. Although I can hear the caller in "real time," I have to lip-sign my replies and have someone speak them into the telephone. My answers thus take a long time and callers often lose the conversational context of my response. Unless the caller has been informed that I cannot speak and knows that I must use a lip-reading translator, the exchange can quickly become disorganized. I once got a call from a dean of a private university in California asking about a former student of mine. She had applied for a teaching position there. The conversation, after two exchanges, disintegrated into the dean asking if something was wrong with me. He could not understand why I could not talk on the phone directly, even though my student assistant had explained when she answered the phone that I suffered from a neurological condition and could not speak. The dean accused me of using an "artifice" and said he could not converse like this. Perhaps this is why my former student did not get the job.

Even friends who know I cannot speak often get lost talking with me on the phone. I well remember a good friend telling me, "I cannot see my own hand in this conversation." I was crushed. I have not spoken with him by telephone for six years. Even though I have the urge to call, I avoid it.

I talk on the phone to a limited number of people. They are my children and my few slow-talking friends. One of the easiest people to talk to is John O'Neill, a sociologist and longtime friend in Toronto. He is an Englishman and has a slow, considered way of talking. He knows in detail my difficulties in speaking, having stayed at my house.

Now that I have such problems using the phone, I think back to the time when calling was a natural habit. I was on the phone throughout the day at work and at home. Such talk was the main avenue of maintaining relationships with people at funding agencies in Washington, D.C. The phone is essential in winning grants and keeping up on funding programs, hopefully before your competition finds out. Phone talk is vital in maintaining and continuing friendships, too. I used to make regular rounds of calls to friends who I had not seen in a week or two.

The Hard Work of Interaction

Being increasingly alone during the course of my illness has thrown many things once taken for granted into relief. I have learned by disappointment and frustration, as well by reflection, that being with people takes a lot of bodily, socially concerted work. I no longer have the capacity to move effortlessly from office to office, chatting there and in the halls. I cannot pick up the phone and easily converse with friends, relatives, and colleagues. I cannot travel, making new friends and sustaining old work relations, seeing my older children in California, and participating in professional meetings. My morning medical care routines make early socializing impossible. I am fed through a tube: lunches are out, and I go to very few dinners.

I have a difficult time manipulating my body appropriately when I am in my wheelchair and see persons with whom I want to converse. I cannot schedule my body movements, including my speech, to recognizably hail interlocutors and open up and then sustain a conversation. My ineptitude at normal communication is generalized, as indicated in this overheard remark: "He has so much difficulty on the path that I don't want to see him in his office. It is too painful." The witnessed problems I have with managing my body in producing my part in the recognizable, socially concerted routines of interaction are seen as indicative of a larger, underlying pattern of troubles, involvement in which would be uncomfortable for interlocutors.

I no longer embody the practices of easily being with people. I exhibit, especially when I am in my wheelchair, body movement limitations that are representative of a wider, underlying bed of interactional embarrassments. I no longer occupy the chat lines in offices, restaurants, meetings, and parties that produce invitations and counterinvitations. The phone is no longer a practical instrument. I do not travel. In short, I am not embedded in the thick format of face-to-face conversation that produces being in proximal contact with others.

I miss the close company of friends, colleagues, students, and others. However, isolation has its benefits. In the past, the number of hours spent socializing was enormous. I did not have the discipline to set time aside for academic work. Now, because of my relative isolation and because of my shortened work day, I have the discipline of a drill instructor. I get far more work done in a week than I accomplished in a month before my illness. The opportunity to think out problems in a sustained fashion is a normal routine now. This, I really enjoy.

Aside from the opportunity to think, an unexpected benefit of isolation is that I am able to be with my family more. If I were a normal, successful full professor, I would be constantly traveling to professional meetings, to funding agencies, and to visit colleagues doing the same kind of work. Because of my paralysis, I have found another way to be successful. At the same time, I can enjoy being around my family, too.

6 Tragic Narratives

In 1982 I was swimming at a beach in Southern Leyte, not far from where General Douglas MacArthur landed in his now fabled return to the Philippines in World War II. I was with my wife and a close friend from Honolulu, Boyd Slomoff. Boyd and I got into a typical male competition about who could swim the farthest out from the beach. There were two mooring buoys for ships about two hundred yards off shore. Boyd swam out first to the large white buoys. I followed and found him hanging off a buoy, panting with exhaustion. There was a strong current, and each of us had to swim against it to the west, then turn toward the buoy after we had passed it. Boyd left the buoy first and swam back to the beach, letting the current drag him to the east.

I waited at the buoy, just as exhausted as Boyd. I watched him make it to the beach, about a quarter mile from where we had our towels. When I finally started toward the shore, the high tide had ebbed and the current to the east, to the Pacific, had substantially increased. When I got ten feet out from the buoy I started to slide to the east at a much faster rate than had Boyd. No matter how hard I swam against the current and the ebbing tide, I found myself being pulled eastward. For every two feet of progress toward the beach I was dragged ten feet to the east.

I saw a Shell petroleum products pier down the beach. The current and tide were dragging me to it. I did not want to get caught up in the pier's pilings, which were soaked in oil and tar. As I was swept down the beach and moved closer and closer to the pier, I became frightened and began to struggle against the current, only to get leg cramps. I decided to relax, avoid the cramps, and float to the sticky pier. As I neared the pilings, Divina had discovered my difficulties and ran down to the water's edge, yelling at me to swim to the beach. Her shouts attracted the attention of two fishermen in a Filipino-style outrigger canoe. They followed my wife's pointing and paddled near me. The men told me to hang on the side of the canoe as they brought me to shore. I had come within ten feet of the black pier.

Swimming off Leyte

Recently my nine-year-old son, Thomas, won an art competition for drawing a picture symbolizing Hawaii. The picture was put on the side of Northwest Airlines' Promotional Worldplane, along with decals of paintings by other child art contest winners in Asia and the United States to celebrate the airline's fifty years of trans-Pacific service. There was a ceremony at the Honolulu airport, where Thomas was placed on a hydraulic lift and was raised up to sign the enlargement of his picture on the side of the 747. After the signing, there was a televised ceremony in which Thomas donated the five thousand dollars Northwest Airlines had given him to the Hawaii Muscular Dystrophy Association. We lined up before the cameras of every television station in Honolulu and my son, holding a huge cardboard check from the airline, handed it to a representative of the association. When the representative took the check, she said in a very loud voice, "This is for people like Thomas's dad, who suffers from Lou Gehrig's disease. Thank you very much, Thomas." When the woman pronounced me a victim of Lou Gehrig's disease, I felt caught up in a strong current, as strong as the one I had encountered in Leyte fifteen years before.

Except for their accounts of the ancient Hawaiians, contemporary residents of the islands are not aware that their talk is the primary means of producing and reproducing social structure. When the woman uttered "This is for people like Thomas's dad, who suffers from Lou Gehrig's disease," I could only think of the dreadful things people associate with the name Lou Gehrig. The category "Lou Gehrig" is an intersubjective one, known in common appellation; it constantly enters into the social fabric by the old Gary Cooper movie, by television advertisements featuring Lou Gehrig in a baseball uniform, by a contemporary player breaking his consecutive-game record, by jokes on sitcoms, by movies about Lou Gehrig, and by stories in newspapers and magazines about the tragic deaths of the rich and famous from the disease that bears his name.

The category "Lou Gehrig" is like many illness categories. Once it has become an objective feature of your biography, others inspect your present qualities for how they reveal what is the assumed end: death. This is a documentary method of interpretation, where the presuppositions or background expectations about disease and how the presence of signs and symptoms is read project the future of an individual. We do this projective reading every time we see a grossly obese stranger or a person who has what is colloquially called a "beep-beep" nose. The obesity projects heart attack or stroke; the red, blotchy nose with broken capillaries connotes cirrhosis. The obese and alcoholics may live for many years, but Lou Gehrig's disease carries the expectation of the swift loss of motor control and death by respiratory failure in three years. In Lou Gehrig's disease, as in many cancers, the end is near.

Here I was, sitting in my wheelchair beneath the glare of the TV lights, and the lady from the Hawaii Muscular Dystrophy Association says in the loudest voice, "This is for people like Thomas' Dad, who suffers from Lou Gehrig's disease." I felt as if the aura of spoiled identity had descended on me. As with the current in Leyte, try as I might, I was carried away by the woman's remarks. After her utterance, the cameras moved away from me and I noticed that everyone in the room averted their gaze. If appearing at a ceremony in a wheelchair, in a paralyzed body, had been difficult for me, I was now an official outcast.

I have always resisted the label Lou Gehrig's disease. When neurologists, after audible sighs, would tell me their diagnoses, I knew I bore a strong stigma. There are other names for the same disease: ALS, or amyotrophic lateral sclerosis, is one; motor neuron disease is another. Today, ALS is used almost as frequently as Lou Gehrig's disease. There is an ALS organization based in Los Angeles, with an accompanying newsletter; there are ALS research meeting postings and bulletin boards on the World Wide Web. I prefer the more socially ambiguous term motor neuron disease. It does not suggest the short, stigmatizing time horizon of Lou Gehrig's disease or ALS. Most persons do not know what motor neuron disease is about, and when they hear the words, they take little notice.

Health Talk

I am now engaged in a study of multidisciplinary rounds in a teaching hospital. We have completed one phase of the work and are in the middle of the other. The first phase was an exploratory ethnography to get a feel of the social interaction of rounds. The second is a videotaping of naturally occurring medical rounds conversation. The ethnographic field notes and an inspection of the videos illustrate the same thing. The participants in rounds conversations appear to be unreflective about how utterances like "His lungs are shot and he is on his last legs," "She has congestive heart failure and we better see that she has a living will," and "Cancer has riddled his body *but he is so mean he won't die!*" structure and predicate ongoing and subsequent interaction, including dimensions of direct patient care. The rounds conversants are like my in-laws, who, when they fight, say, "It is only words." It is as if utterances are regarded as neutral phenomena, having limited or no impact on the present interaction. There are many strange twists and turns, as well as logical inconsistencies, in cultural practices. One of the logical dilemmas of culture (and it seems to be cross-cultural) is that although actors expect and believe their talk and body behavior affect their interlocutors, producing further talk and body movement, at the same time these actors stand ready to exempt their talk and behavior from having any effect at all. This can be seen in such phrases as "It is only talk," "I did not mean it," "I don't know what I am talking about," "I am just thinking out loud," and "Do what I do, not what I say."

When I inspected field notes and partial transcripts of the research on collaborative rounds and when I later viewed videotapes of the rounds, two things caught my attention. The first was the repeated talk among nurses that selected physicians were continuing to treat patients who would soon die. Mention of physicians who would not give up on their patients was a source of complaint, as in: "Why is he treating her? He is avoiding the inevitable. She is going to die."

The other thing that was noticeable in the field notes and in the videotapes was the speaking behavior of a social worker involved. Every time the nurses would engage in what they called "death talk," the social worker would insert a remark about getting a living will from the patient. She would ask, "Does he have a living will?" If the answer was no, the social worker would say, "I will talk to the patient about getting him to sign a living will." Sometimes, she would say, "I will get one."

Such conversations color subsequent interaction, setting up possibilities for conversational predication and further bodily behavior such as audible exhaling, sighing, rolling of the eyes, and other signs of dispreference for the patient. I can testify to this kind of conversation and bodily signification from my nearly three months in the intensive care unit. When I was close to death, the amount of bodily-signed dispreference for being in my company was overwhelming. When I started to recover, I would routinely witness the nurses talking in my room, speaking "death talk" about patients in nearby rooms. When I questioned the nurses about these conversations they would normally respond, "It is just talk and a way of relieving pressure." When I did not seem satisfied with this, some would say, "We don't mean anything by it." A few would remark, "Don't listen to us. We are just a bunch of crazy ladies talking."

Unintended Subtleties

There is more to damaging talk than yelling out my diagnosis on Hawaiian and Japanese television, the "death talk" of nurses, the bodily signs of dispreference, and a social worker's fixation with getting a living will. I am not speaking to the direct affront, as when a male nurse from a nursing agency, who was caring for me at home, remarked, "If I had what you have, I would be better off dead." Rather, the denigrations I want to address are much more subtle and usually not intended. The denigrating remarks emanate from the common culture about disability.

The comments come in many forms. Some appear in letters, cards, and Christmas greetings. Some come in newspaper stories about me and my heroic family. Some are passed along in casual conversation. Some are performed by bodily gestures. I will address the written comments first.

My family and I receive many Christmas cards from my relatives and my wife's relatives. There is always a written message, especially from my oldest aunt, who mentions that she continuously prays for me. Frequently, Divina's aunts write the same message, adding that they are praying for her, too. Although it is nice to be on others' minds and feel them pulling for you, to hear repeatedly that you are the subject of a request for divine intervention is a bit tiring. I say tiring, as much as I appreciate the prayers, because it is the only form of message I receive from the well-intentioned aunts. Being always and only addressed as the subject of prayers limits who I am and focuses my attention on myself as a person of pity.

Attached to the written messages about prayer are consoling appreciations of how hard our life has been and will be. This is when the enormity of prejudice in the commonsense culture about disabled persons can be felt. An example is "I know every day is a struggle and I wish I could be there to help you both." Another variation, directed at my wife, "I know this is not what you expected, but the Lord has a different mission for each of us." Still another is "You have given up so much and still you accomplish so much." And last, "I don't know how you do it."

These appreciations of "our situation" topicalize, circulate, and reproduce the notion that I, as a physically dependent disabled individual, have made life difficult and at times unbearable for myself and my family. Divina will often say, "Ask anyone and they will tell us how hard our life is." It is not that our life does not have difficulties, but the frequent conversational and written topicalizing of them reifies those difficulties, letting them hang over our heads, ever ready for speech. The extension of the topicality of our hardship, a continuous proffering of the subject for conversation, also comes in letters and e-mail. The pervasiveness of remarks about our "difficulties" and "having given up so much," and the ubiquity of such sentiments as "You have lost everything," "I don't know how you both do it," "If we could bottle your courage, we could be rich," and "If I were you, I would have given up long ago," build a palpable wall of social structure to which my wife and I must be accountable.

Honolulu Star-Bulletin

On July 20, 1994, the afternoon newspaper in Honolulu ran a front-page story on me, "Disabled UH Professor Fights to Work, Love, Hope"; the subhead noted, "He Battles a Disease." The story featured a large color photo of me sitting in my office chair, with one of my research assistants at the computer keyboard. The photo was taken from above, displaying me with my head hanging to my right and looking up at the photographer through the top of my glasses. It was not a straight-on photograph of my face.

Most people are happy when they get a story about themselves in the local newspaper. I was afraid from the start that my tale would be one of tragedy. I avoided the newspapers for years, thinking I did not want to further the language and topicality of the tragic lives of disabled persons and their families. Finally, I relented and accepted the opportunity for a feature story, arranged by the press officer of the university's Social Science Research Institute. I told the reporter that I did not want a story on the order of "look at what happened to Britt and his poor family."

Nevertheless, the feature was framed in tragedy. On the first page, the one with the photograph of me in a cockeyed position, I was described as having my muscles "wasted." "Since 1989," the story went on, "he has had virtually no muscle control, causing him to slump in his wheelchair. He cannot move his hands, arms or fingers." There followed a litany of what I cannot do, eat, drink, and speak. Then the story shifted to how I am dependent on my translators for my productivity and my ability to assist in my own care. Then it told, from the viewpoint of colleagues, how I once was "young, aggressive, bright, pushy, hardworking and smart" but now have become a heroic figure, struggling to live life to its fullest. The tragedy angle is exemplified in the two last paragraphs: "Robillard was near death in 1991, when he developed pneumonia. He knows he is vulnerable, but chooses to cling to his chances to work, love and hope. 'I don't think of death,' he said. 'I think of what I have to do tomorrow or next week.'"

The tragedy of what happened to Britt Robillard is a weak sister, though, to the tragedy of what happened to his wife, Divina. In an accompanying story, "Caring for Husband a Full-Time Job," I am described as "motionless in my wheelchair" and requiring attention that has put my wife's career and doctorate on "hold." The reporter notes how we have become isolated as a couple and as a family from visiting with friends and from traveling.

The capstone to the tragedy is the revelation that the demands of my care and my reportedly protesting care by others has led my wife to depression and a necessary change in attitude where, she says, "I put my foot down." Divina is described as needing a break. There is a statement about my wife worrying that my condition may worsen and that she may not be able to take care of me; she knows I would not last long outside the home, meaning in an institution. The last paragraph reads: "We like to sit and be quiet together . . . to just share the silences."

My point here is not that the story has no basis in fact. Life for the disabled and their families is, indeed, fraught with difficulties. My argument, rather, is that a story formed around the narrative of tragedy and solely tragedy perpetuates the largely unexamined commonsense notions that disabled individuals are in decline, with wasted muscles, slouched in their wheelchairs, and that they are angry, demanding, mean, and nonresponsive to the needs of others. Reproducing these stock-tragic figures in newspaper stories, in conversations that tacitly reference this commonsense version of disabled people, in cards, letters, and prayers builds a self-ratifying, stigmatizing, and highly limiting conception of the individual.

We may think, in the era of the Americans with Disabilities Act, the manufacture of a wheelchair Barbie doll, and the appearance of persons in wheelchairs in many advertising campaigns, that the unexamined, commonsense assumptions about disabled individuals no longer exist. Yet, the repeated use of the commonsense text in letters, cards, public declarations of my diagnosis, and newspaper stories is overwhelming evidence that the text is alive and well. It is repeated in casual conversations between my wife and her female friends, between my wife and her mother. It is broadcast around the world every time CNN runs a story on the disabled and their suffering families. It is reproduced endlessly.

Let me give further support for my description of the unexamined, commonsense background assumptions about the disabled. In the *Honolulu Star-Bulletin* story there are two mentions of my sitting in a wheelchair. In one, I sat "slouched"; in the other, I sat "motionless." In point of fact, I never sat in a wheelchair during the interview with the reporter. Nor did I sit in my wheelchair during the newspaper photo sessions at my office or my house. Neither the reporter nor the photographer saw me in my wheelchair. I did not mention my wheelchair in the interview. I find wheelchairs uncomfortable and transfer out of them as soon as I arrive at the office or at home. I use a normal office chair for work and a lounge chair at home.

The fact that the reporter, Linda Hosek, did not see me in my wheelchair or hear me or anyone else speak of the ten minutes a day I spend in it, but nonetheless used the figure of me in a wheelchair, is testament to the commonsense typifications about disabled people and their co-categorization with wheelchairs. Formulations such as "wheelchair-bound" and "confined to a wheelchair" are extremely strong categories and are almost synonymous with disabled persons. That the concept "wheelchair" was used, absent any supporting evidence whatsoever, is incidental. If it does not have verification in fact, it has stronger verification in commonsense. The countless conversational exchanges about wheelchair-bound people, as well as the rest of the characterizations about being angry and demanding, socially institutionalize and verify these speech narratives. The case is similar to what many residents of Hawaii say about Samoans: "Samoans are . . . " Even though such utterances are made by persons who do not know a single Samoan, they acquire and maintain social currency and validity merely by repetitive conversational use.

The Myth of Sexual Dysfunction

As when the reporter used the figure of me "slouched" and "motionless" in my wheelchair, despite not having seen me in a wheelchair, my paralysis leads people to think that I have lost sexual function. It does not matter that my penis is one of the last things working properly. I still experience this assumption, seemingly part of the omniprevalent condition of paralytics. The assumption comes, I think, from the widespread commonsense knowledge about patients with spinal cord injuries, even though this knowledge, as Christopher Reeve and others report, is often inaccurate. This assumption about loss of sexual function, no matter what the diagnosis, is an ideal that assembles what the perceiver sees.

One day my wife had an adverse reaction to a muscle relaxant she was taking. She experienced difficulty standing and became dizzy. She called an ambulance. The crew came to the house and to my bedroom, where Divina explained what was happening to her.

One of the ambulance crew seized on my disability and started, on the drive to the hospital, to say that my wife was worn out and needed time away from me. He proposed to provide the respite by meeting with her for coffee. A week later, he called to arrange a date. Divina told him she was not interested and not to call the house again. We were both shocked that a county employee could use supposedly confidential medical information to call someone for a date.

My wife tells me that as soon as they know that she has a paralyzed husband in a wheelchair many men start making advances. She thinks they are motivated by commonsense thinking that she is sex starved. Having a paralyzed husband leads many men to assume that "she is not getting enough" and is an easy mark. These advances come all the time.

Divina was prompted to think of the commonsense idealizations about paralytic men and their wives by a remark from the wife of a colleague. The wife asked her why she did not divorce me when I became paralyzed. My wife started to think of all the commonsense assumptions about me in my paralytic state and the many levels of assumptions about our life together, which combine to motivate questions like that and the sexual advances. Divina, a good sociologist, suggested that I put it in the book.

7 Bionic Man

Coupled with the institutions of individualism is the widespread belief in technological progress and the belief that almost any problem has a technological fix. I do not know how many times I have been told, jokingly or not, "We are going to make you into a bionic man."

This chapter is about the almost omniprevalent social pressure to obtain and use computers and other assistive devices. I am reminded of this pressure every time I see a television commercial for a particular brand of hearing aid. The ad features two characters, a grandfather and granddaughter, getting ready to go on a fishing trip. There is a setup conversation where the girl asks, "What time is it?" The granddaughter reflects that she did not talk to her grandfather much before because he could not hear. Then the grandfather chimes in, continuing the reflective time-out, saying something on the order of "I couldn't hear what she was saying. But now I can hear everything, and it was a shame I didn't help myself sooner. I was missing out and could have helped myself." The ad rejoins "real time" when the grandfather answers her question, saying, "It is near five." They jump in a four-door sports vehicle and drive off on the presumed fishing trip.

This commercial is often run late in the afternoon on CNN. It targets elderly Americans who watch *Early Prime,* an hour of news aimed at "those in the prime of life."

Helping Yourself

Note that the grandfather mentions helping himself twice. Helping yourself is often synonymous with, or the same as, one of the most glorified cultural ideals of late-twentieth-century America: independence. After finding a physician who would manage my condition without telling me to take ample amounts of Valium, get psychological counseling, get my affairs in order, or retire to a time where I would get ready to die, as my first doctor did, I was sent to the Rehabilitation Hospital of the Pacific. There I went through a speech evaluation and occupational and physical therapy assessments.

Speech therapy was first. I will always remember the frown of disapproval on the speech therapist's face as I failed one speech assessment after another. She told me I had a collapsed upper palate and would never recover. The therapist seemed particularly officious when she told Divina and me that the lip-signing and lip-reading system we had fashioned on our own was inefficient. She assumed no one could learn it and I would be restricted in communication if I did not acquire an artificial voice. "You know, no one will understand you. You will be dependent on your wife and mother-in-law. Don't you want to be independent?"

I was dismissed from the presence of the speech therapist with this question. I had no opportunity to respond. I wanted to tell her that my wife and mother-in-law were not the only or even the best lip readers available to me. I could not make eye contact with my mother-in-law, who had accompanied me to the hospital. Failing to summon her to serve as a lip-reading translator, I felt myself being wheeled backward out of the speech therapist's room by the physical therapist, who had assumed a managerial role in getting me from one section of the hospital to another. I could not see or turn my body to address the wheelchair pusher behind me. I was off to the occupational therapist, the physical therapist announced as we backed out of the speech therapist's office.

I was pleased to see the smiling face of the occupational therapist. She was sitting at a big table in a large room. The room was also used for physical therapy. Across from the occupational therapy table were four cushioned platforms, slightly elevated, used for physical therapy. The platforms were busy, with persons either doing exercises or being transferred to or from wheelchairs. The physical therapist, my pusher, placed me sitting across the table from the occupational therapist, with my back to the platforms.

I would spend more time with the pleasant, nonjudgmental occupational therapist than I would with the speech therapist. I still had some movement in my left arm, and I would do arm and finger exercises as she smiled and made small talk. I used to look forward to my sessions with the occupational therapist.

Evidently, the occupational and speech therapists had crossed paths, most probably in a case meeting. The occupational therapist, with the assistance of a hovering salesman from the local branch of a national medical supply house, began to expose me to a series of artificial-voice machines. The first one is memorable to this day, eleven years later. Designed for children who had full mobility of their arms and hands, it was a platform or board on which a series of pressure-sensitive boxes were located. One would press a box and a voice would say a message: "I have to urinate," "I am cold," "You are hurting me," "I want to go to bed," "I am hungry," "Please call my mother," "I want to talk now," "Please do not do that," and so on.

Even though the machine had a limited capacity to add various phrases, for me it suffered from four glaring drawbacks. The first was that I had limited use of my spastic left arm. Very weak, it would shake uncontrollably, and it took an exhausting effort to extend my arm. I attempted to work the device by trying to push the panels to set off the individual phrases. I had a difficult time pushing one voice panel and could not control my arm to push it a second time. The one I had pushed uttered, "Please do not do that."

The second problem was that the limited number of voice panels and accompanying utterances would not permit a topical response to an ongoing conversation. Pushing the panels for "I have to urinate," "I want to go to bed," "I want to talk now," and the like produces only initiatory comments. These are of limited utility in responding to the formulations of others. You cannot keep repeating "I want to go to bed" in a moving conversation without appearing to have lost your mind.

The third drawback is the limited vocabulary of the device and the simple-request nature of the statements. This made me feel like an infant, unable to respond to and participate in the contingent, ongoing development of conversational topics. Some persons have suggested that normal-bodied people will take account of your speech impairment and your use of an artificial voice and give you the leeway to converse with them. As noted in Chapter 3, my experience does not bear out this generous statement. Furthermore, such statements do not stem from a systematic examination of conversation (see Goodwin 1981; Atkinson and Heritage 1984; Sacks 1995; Psathas 1995).

The final difficulty is that when you are searching for the appropriate phrase in this machine, or any artificial-voice device, you must avert your gaze from the person you are trying to talk with. Should readers doubt the importance of gaze in interaction, I ask them to systematically avert their gaze while talking to people, especially at the beginning of their turn to speak. If this does not have a disorganizing effect on the conversation, I ask the experimenters to heighten the stakes by exhibiting some visible stigma (Goffman 1963). In my experience, the more serious the visible stigma in the disabled interactant, the more likely the aversion of gaze by that person is to end or at the least confuse the conversation. The study of gaze is neglected in sociology (Frankel 1983).

I announced my reservations about the artificial-voice machine. It was immediately agreed that I did not have the physical ability to depress the appropriate voice panels accurately and repeatedly. My objections about being unable to participate in the contingent flow of topics and the other drawbacks I found were not considered seriously. The discussion quickly turned to making some device that would permit me to press the voice panels—a stick that I would hold in my mouth and a puff-and-blow mechanism were suggested as replacements for my hands.

I wondered about the memories of the therapists. The speech therapist had told her colleagues and me that I could not speak because my upper palate had fallen, had no muscle tone, and had lost the ability to close off my oral cavity from my nose. Yet, here were the same people recommending a puff-and-blow tube, when they had told me three weeks earlier that I could not close off my nose from my mouth. I could not blow with my mouth because the air from my lungs would go out my nose.

Using a stick in my mouth was also unworkable. I was told, and my experience confirmed, that I had poor and progressively deteriorating muscle control of my oral cavity.

The speech, occupational, and physical therapists had explained to me that I had a bulbar condition that led me to produce an extra amount of saliva. I would think they could infer, from their demonstrated knowledge of my lack of oral control and the saliva problem, that a stick in my mouth would not work. I will address this apparent lack of inferential reasoning in the conclusion of this chapter, where I discuss routine grounds of the body's capability.

After I had explained that the voice panel board would not work for me, I got the distinct impression, mainly from facial expressions of the therapists, the salesman, and my wife, that I was being willfully obstructive in rejecting the machine. "Don't you want to help yourself?" the salesman asked with a sigh. Divina added, "He is very stubborn." Still, I insisted that the machine was inappropriate.

Scanner

The next time I arrived at the Rehab Hospital the therapists had a new communication machine for me to try. It was far more complex than the first one, being composed of thirty-six separate cells, each with its own utterance. The machine worked by scanning each cell on the board. This was indicated by a light coming on in each cell in a series. You would watch the serial scanning of the lights, and press a foot or hand switch when the light of the message cell you wanted to execute came on; the machine would verbalize the message associated with the cell. You had to watch the serial scanning of lights across the rows of cells, and anticipate the lighting of the cell you wanted.

The cells, coded with numbers and letters, related to a specific message or utterance. I easily memorized the codes and messages for the first five cells. I was not so sure of the next five. Memorizing the cells and trying the ones I could not remember, randomly seeing what they said, was great fun. I thought this machine was much more sophisticated than the first, but it was also much more expensive.

I played with the voice cell machine for about an hour, wondering how I could afford it. I was financially strapped at the time. While I was playing with the scanner the salesman who had brought it busied himself with electric wheelchairs for other patients. When he came over to ask how I liked the machine, I was so immersed in anticipating the scanning sequence of the lights that I could not hear his inquiry. My mother-in-law had to walk in front of me and finally had to speak in a loud voice to get my attention. I had taken theoretical exception to the nonavailability of gaze with the first machine. But now, without plans for doing so, I had got so lost in monitoring the sequence of flickering lights that I could not see or hear the salesman's solicitations. When I explained this operational feature to him, the salesman said, "When you get used to it, you don't have to look at it." He pointed out that you can set the "dwell time," the length of time the light stays on, for each cell. "It takes a month or two to get used to the flickering lights and to learn the best timing for you," he added.

I did not believe the salesman's claim that I would not have to look at the scanner once I had got used to it. I could not figure out how to avoid random voicings when I was not following the sequence of flickering lights. I rejected further consideration of this machine, just as I had with the voice panel version. The only resource I had to initiate and maintain conversation was my gaze. I found I could not raise my voice or interpose my body in front of my interlocutors. I had only my gaze, and even this was often insufficient to hold their attention.

When I decided to let the scanner pass, the salesman, predictably, said, "I am only here to help you help yourself."

Computer Lab at Michigan State

I had worked in the College of Medicine at Michigan State University. When I lived in faculty housing in East Lansing, I met an interesting colleague who was both a linguist and an electrical engineer. We had become good friends. I had seen his laboratory and some of the specially designed computers he had made for cerebral palsy clients. I was quite amazed at his design of artificial speech for the specific situation of each client. After my experience with the speech machines at the hospital, I telephoned my friend.

When I called, he asked me to make a videotape of my circumstances. The tape I sent him showed me working at the computer with my research assistants. I also had myself taped as I transferred from my car to my office in my wheelchair.

When he called back he suggested I get a speaking computer to be mounted on my wheelchair. I told him I only use my wheelchair to go from the car to the office and back. (This assumption that I am in it all day is universal.) I explained that my folding wheelchair is very uncomfortable and that it was beyond me why people expected me to remain there throughout the day.

My friend quickly told me that I should obtain a more comfortable wheelchair, one that did not fold up, and buy a van to transport it and myself. I explained, as I would do countless times, that I did not have the money to buy a van. I also pointed out that the wheelchair I was using had been bought by the local chapter of the Muscular Dystrophy Association; its purchase had been arranged for by the hospital through its special, almost monopolistic, relationship with a medical supply house. There was no competitive shopping for the chair that I had. We were shown no other models.

My friend next advised me to get funding for a new chair and a van from a foundation. There are two kinds of assumptions about disabled people, even on the part of professionals who work with them every day. The first is that there is either money to spend on equipment or that spending priorities can and will be reshuffled to make it available. The second is that there is an unlimited supply of private and public money for purchasing equipment. The first assumption is fueled by a background expectation that you should buy whatever equipment will make you more self-sufficient and less of a burden on caretakers. This is another version of the "help yourself" nostrum in the hearing aid commercials.

There is always a tension between the financial demands of those who are constantly encouraging you to buy equipment to make life and communication easier and better, in theory, and the ongoing financial responsibilities to the household, including children. The mortgage must be paid, whether you are disabled or not. Expenses for food, house maintenance, kids' tuition and books, insurance, car bills, and the rest do not go away because you are disabled. There are no financial exemptions for the sick, even though prevailing sociological theory, since Talcott Parsons, stipulates that social expectations are suspended for them. The constant barrage of requests to purchase assistive equipment to help yourself and your family makes you feel inadequate at first for not having the necessary funds. This feeling of inadequacy quickly turns to anger.

Those urging you to buy assistive equipment often use the refrain, "It is much cheaper for your employer and the state to keep you productive and paying taxes by buying you equipment." Even though my employer, the University of Hawaii, has been more than generous in buying me a computer program (described below), there are severe limits to what can be done with public money. Because of my professor's salary, I do not qualify for state assistance in the purchase of equipment. Some private groups, such as the Muscular Dystrophy Association, will buy basic equipment like wheelchairs. But this assistance is limited to the basics. There is a dearth of state and private assistance for the disabled, something you do not find out until you yourself are disabled.

My friend from Michigan State knew a woman who was coming to Honolulu for a convention. She worked in special education near Detroit and had also worked with him in equipping young students suffering from cerebral palsy with wheelchair-mounted computer speech synthesizers.

This engaging woman brought an interesting alarm switch that was controlled by a light beam. She also brought a number of catalogs of commercially available equipment. One of the computer programs in the catalogs reviewed by my friend, the Freewheel program, would be recommended for me.

The Infrared Pointer

When I was hospitalized in 1991 for pneumonia, a colleague bought me a laptop computer, a Toshiba, with a monochrome display. I had earlier purchased a program called Freewheel, which was prominently featured in a newsletter on assistive devices I received from my friend at Michigan State.

Freewheel consisted of an on-screen keyboard, an infrared beam, and a glass reflector that permitted the infrared beam to be focused on a letter or function key on the keyboard displayed on the monitor. If you held the reflected beam on a letter key, the machine would type the letter. The amount of time you had to hold the reflected beam on the key could be varied or changed. The keyboard display on the monitor covered much of the screen, permitting, at most, the display of three typed lines.

I tried Freewheel for two months, with a separate color monitor. I had trouble holding the reflected beam steady and did not have enough neck strength to hold my head still. I also found the infrared beam to be unsteady even when an able-bodied person used it. I had to concentrate on the monitor, lest the bouncing beam reflect on the wrong letter, typing it and requiring a repair job. Besides the total focus required on the monitor, another problem was that I could see only three lines of text. When I am writing, I must see the previous paragraph or two to determine where my argument or logic is going. I also constantly reread what I wrote and just as constantly change the phrasing of the argument. I could not do this with Freewheel.

I had the vendor install my favorite word-processing program and Freewheel on the laptop. The vendor had been recommended by the hospital's social worker. The social worker had heard from Divina that I had a program that was head operated. Divina had told the social worker that I had a speech synthesizer to go with the head-operated input system. She had also mentioned that we were never able to get the Freewheel system to operate successfully and had no idea how to hook it up. Thus, the owner of the computer store from which the laptop had been purchased was brought forth to end my program installation problems. Not only would he sell us the laptop, he would install the programs and the speech synthesizer; in addition, he would solve operational difficulties as we went along.

But there was a problem with the vendor, one of which we were not aware when he brought the new laptop to my hospital room. He was on the verge of going out of business. When he presented the computer, and received payment, he asked for the program disks and the speech synthesizer, which he promised to install and de-bug. He said it would take a week. The week soon turned into a month. The colleague involved in the purchase tried to call the computer store. The number on his business card had been disconnected. The colleague called information and was told there was no listing under either the name of the store or the name of the owner.

This sort of problem is common. Helping the disabled with unique solutions to situational problems is not a mass market proposition. The return on capital is low and the labor is intensive. Either persons do the helping work on assistive devices for disabled individuals as a sideline, or else their help and the devices are priced at their real market value, out of the reach of those with moderate incomes.

There were numerous problems with the Freewheel program. First, there was the instability of the pointer on the monitor screen. I altered the pointer's dwell time, but this did not stabilize it. Second, also as mentioned earlier, I could not see enough text to follow the development of my writing. Third, I was then using Note Bene, a wonderful word-processing program designed for academic writers; the Freewheel program did not work efficiently with it, however. Fourth, there was the question of where to place the infrared beam projector when working with the laptop. We had been using a full-screen monitor before, putting the projector on top of it (The literature accompanying the Freewheel program indicated that it was designed for use with a cathoderay monitor.) We needed a stable platform on which to place the projector, one that could easily be moved. The vendor promised to construct a portable platform. Fifth, and finally, the voice synthesizer that I had purchased to work with Freewheel remained a total mystery. No one knew how to make it work.

I was soon discharged from the hospital. My immediate concern was getting back to work. I already had an effective way of communicating there, by lip-signing and lip-reading. I felt the pressure of the doubts that some of my closest colleagues had about my ever being able to be productive again. Returning to work became my overriding objective.

I did not worry about the laptop, despite not having solved its problems. However, most of my caregivers in the hospital, shortly before I was released, expressed disappointment that it did not work. A number of them said, "I thought you would be talking up a storm by now." They inquired, "What happened to the laptop?" I would tell them, using a spelling board, "The computer man disappeared." They would commiserate and offer their hope that "the people at the university can figure it out."

The Department of Special Education, and Engineering Students

I would sporadically try to use Freewheel in my office, employing my tabletop computer. I found these attempts frustrating. As time went on, and particularly as my workload grew beyond what it had been before my hospitalization, I stopped trying to use the program.

I had worked on writing a grant for a rehabilitation research and demonstration center for the University of Hawaii Medical School and had met many faculty in the Department of Special Education and the Department of Counseling in the College of Education. About six months after I had returned to work in the summer of 1991, the chairman of the Department of Special Education asked me to become a board member of the University Affiliated Programs on Developmental Disabilities. Not wanting to be wheeled around campus to attend meetings, I wrote a letter to the head of Special Education, asking if some meetings could be held in my building. The executive director of the University Affiliated Programs answered the letter. He phoned my office and asked to come over for a chat.

The executive director was new to Hawaii. He had been hired on a new grant. I was expecting him to talk about how I could be involved in developing research for the University Affiliated Programs. However, he opened the conversation by saying, "How can we help you?" I replied, "You can have the meetings in this building." He then said, "I mean how can we bring our resources on developmental disabilities to make your life easier?" I immediately went back to my motive for writing the letter. He acknowledged the letter but said, "First, I want to know how we can use our resources to help you. We can talk about the letter later. If we cannot help you, we are in a poor position to help kids. We have a rich resource base at the university and I would hope you will let us use it for you."

I consented to the apparent wish to make me into a client. At this time, my wife, Divina, was still hovering around me. She was immediately drawn into the conversation and listed standing troubles, such as controlling the television, video cassette recorder, and stereo. We added the problem of turning pages in books, journals, magazines, and student papers. The executive director made a list and said, "I will think of how we can solve these problems and get back to you."

A week later, he called and said he wanted to come over with two undergraduate electrical engineering students and their faculty advisor. They came to the office and talked about controlling the electrical appliances and turning pages. The students measured my body and suggested solutions. They explained they were doing this project to satisfy the requirement that they produce a practical solution to everyday problems. The electrical engineering faculty advisor said one student would work on the electronic controls and the other would work on a page turner. He asked if he could come to our house and take measurements, see what kind of TV we had, and assess our living situation.

The advisor came to the house. We were full of expectations. My wife and I repeatedly told ourselves that the university was the best place to come up with customized solutions to our specific problems. We talked a lot about the underutilization of the university and the amazing array of resources it possessed to solve problems for the disabled. A kind of unbounded enthusiasm descended on us.

The students would come to the office two more times. On the second visit, they brought a baseball cap with a control mechanism on top. The student who was working on the page turner admitted he had come up short and asked my permission to combine his efforts with those of the student working on the controls.

I tried the hat. It worked by the wearer leaning from side to side. If you leaned to the right, it would change the channel on the TV. But it was not consistent. The student who had designed and built it said, "It needs work." We agreed the students would fine-tune the cap-mounted control and come back for another test.

I never saw them again. Divina called the faculty advisor two times and reported that the students had not completed or delivered the control. Each time he responded that he would contact them. But the students did not call or come to the office.

The Consultant

I had Divina call the executive director of the University Affiliated Programs to report that the student volunteers from the Department of Electrical Engineering had disappeared. We also mentioned that we had great hopes and that they were being dashed. The executive director promised to look into it and get back to us.

We never understood what actually happened with his follow-up. He reported that he called the faculty advisor, who said the students had moved on. The executive director apologized and promised to come up with something else.

Four months later, he called the office and said there was someone I should meet, a computer consultant for the disabled.

A man, about forty-five years old and wearing a freshly pressed, expensive aloha shirt, arrived in my office almost immediately. He was accompanied by the executive director, who soon left, explaining he had a meeting and only wanted to make sure the consultant found his way to my office.

The aloha-shirt-clad man stated he was new to Hawaii. He informed us that he worked part-time for a nonprofit business serving the needs of the disabled. He opened a catalog of assistive aids—a commercial catalog developed by a distributor of the equipment. Surprised, I asked if he was a salesman in the guise of a consultant. He flushed and said he was only serving as a guide to equipment. I then asked, "How do you support yourself?" He said he received a commission on sales, but added, "I connect you with the proper technical support for computerized speech and you don't have to pay, except by donation."

I had the impression of being back at the stage where the salesman was trying to sell me equipment at the hospital. The man insisted on showing me the catalog. It was soon evident that he had little technical knowledge of the programs he was urging me to buy. I asked him whether the programs were compatible with Windows or DOS. Although these were simple questions, he replied, "I will get back to you on that."

I tired of him quickly. "I have already seen similar catalogs and I don't have the money to buy," I said "There are ways to finance the purchase," he responded. When I told him I was so broke after my hospitalization that I could not afford a penny, he got up and said, somewhat curtly, "I am only trying to help you help yourself." He offered his business card and left.

The Teaser

I first went to the Muscular Dystrophy Association clinic in 1985. I have been through two doctors there. The first was a physician with whom I had worked at the University of Hawaii School of Medicine. He was a friendly guy who had grown up in the islands and had taken his physical medicine training on the U.S. mainland. He was succeeded by a Chinese doctor from Taiwan.

The Muscular Dystrophy Association paid for my first wheelchair. From time to time I would be called to the MDA clinic to follow up on my condition. The visits were yearly at first, and then several years went by with no visits. In late 1996, I called my former colleague at the School of Medicine to inquire if he knew of any contractors who had experience in bathroom remodeling for the disabled. He told me my file at the MDA clinic listed me as deceased.

The interesting thing about the visits, other than the physical assessments, was that in the course of the conversation both physicians would mention the possibility of acquiring an electric wheelchair. Because this took place in the MDA clinic, there was the reciprocal assumption that the machine would be paid for, in whole or in part, by the MDA. Nothing ever came of the talk about an electric wheelchair. But it was mentioned at the beginning of each clinic visit and peppered the ensuing interaction, almost serving as the functional equivalent of saying "a-hem," a recognized continuing device for conversation. In any case, talking about getting an electric wheelchair opened each clinical encounter, moved us from one phase of the examination to the next, and provided a formal closing to the assessment. I began to suspect that mentioning the machine was a recognized formula for producing an examination.

Ordinarily, the relevant conversation would go like this: "Have you ever thought about an electric wheelchair? It would give you a lot of independence. It would help the person helping you. They would not have to push you around the entire world. It is hard pushing a big person like you. Help those who are helping you. Think about getting an electric wheelchair." Then during the course of the interaction the physician would say, "You have enough neck and head control to operate an electric wheelchair." A similar formulation would be, "They have new controls where you can use your leg to steer and accelerate the chair."

The closing to the clinical assessment would invariably include the following: "You should think about getting an electric wheelchair, if not for yourself, for your wife, who is such a small person." Who would pay for the machine and the vehicle necessary to transport it was never mentioned. (Electric wheelchairs, which cannot be folded into the trunk of a car, require a van.)

I would begin to smile from one corner of my mouth to the other when the comments about an electric wheelchair would start. The physician would see me smiling and say, "He really likes the idea of an electric wheelchair." This formulaic way of reading my smile, and the whole formulaic, repeated discussion of the device, would make me laugh even more. This smiling behavior, in turn, would be assigned the following meaning: "See, he wants one now. You better get him one and life will be so much easier."

There were some other reasons, however, for my laughter. I have absolutely no arm or hand control. My neck and head control is a fable, even though the doctors tell me I can control a wheelchair with a head attachment. My legs are spastic and repeated leg movements quickly tire them. I find it very humorous that the doctors do not know what muscle control I am capable of, that they give me no opportunity to tell them, and that they have no perspective on the financial cost to the household of acquiring an electric wheelchair and transportation for it. The electric wheelchair seems to be an interactional teaser, used by physicians without regard to personal appropriateness and cost.

Words+

I am very lucky to have a good friend who is as near a genius as anyone I have met. We became acquainted in 1963 when we were students in the summer session of the University of California, Berkeley. Dick Post was a promising physics major, who would go on to become a professor. He resigned from MIT to start his own successful high-tech business near Boston.

We kept in touch during and after our undergraduate years. He went to Columbia for his doctorate, and I went to UCLA for mine. We visited one another in graduate school, and he came to see me when I was teaching at Michigan State. His first academic appointment was at the University of Wisconsin, Madison.

After he moved to MIT and I moved to the University of Hawaii, we lost touch. Then one day Dick called the house. Divina informed him of my illness and the limitations on what I could do. Dick was a businessman by then, with many customers in Asia. He promised to visit us on his next trip to Japan and China. He came about a month later.

During the visit he was concerned that he did not have a way of talking to me without a lip-reading translator. He promised to come up with a voice synthesizer. He said I should have the capacity to change TV channels for myself as well. On the next visit, he made a video monitor channel changer. It worked until I broke one of the leg-operated switches during a coughing fit.

About six months later, Dick sent a sample computer disk for a program called Words+. He asked me to try it in my desktop computer, the one I operate by dictating to student assistants. I tried the disk. The apparent problem was that I had no input device for selecting letters and computer program commands.

Dick contacted my closest colleague at the University of Hawaii and arranged for a special switch to be constructed. The idea was to build a splint for my left arm and hand. A switch was placed in the hand area, to be worked by my left pinky finger, which still has some motor control. A local artist, who worked as a Honolulu fireman, built the splint.

It worked very well. However, we learned my pinky soon became fatigued; the switch eventually became fatigued, too, and broke.

Dick is not a patient man. He flew out, determined to make a workable switch. While I was fiddling around about asking the university to purchase the Words+ program, Dick decided his company would buy the program and a state-of-the-art laptop computer. I was very hesitant to ask the university because it had purchased the Freewheel program, which did not work, and because the university was in one of its recurrent fiscal crises.

Dick flew out with a 486 color laptop computer, the Words+ program, a whole bunch of mushroom switches, and a series of room environmental switches for the television, VCR, and lights. He donated the equipment to the university, for my exclusive use. With my cousin Kurt, he constructed a mechanism to hold a head-operated mushroom switch on my easy chair in the family room. The arrangement worked, and I was able to speak by using the Easy-Voice synthesizer attached to the laptop.

Words+ is a sophisticated scanning program with word prediction. A yellow marker scans the individual letters; when it is on the letter you want, you push the mushroom switch, in my case with the side of my head. The program will predict words from the letters you type in. The scanner will highlight the predicted words, and you can use the mushroom switch to click them in. The program saves the words you normally use, adding them to the word prediction dictionary.

Dick wanted to buy a wheelchair mount for the arrangement. But I told him I spend as little time in my wheelchair as possible. I repeated the often-told story about portable wheelchairs being uncomfortable. He accepted that.

I wrote one academic paper with the new laptop. I read many student papers on disk. I jotted many notes to myself on the computer. But I found I did not normally use the Easy-Voice synthesizer. It was my experience that it took so long to set up that by the time I got the device ready to speak my interlocutors had either left the room or the conversation had moved on. This rendered my utterance long out of date and demanded extra efforts to reestablish the context of my remark. Reestablishing the context took so much time, too, that I often found myself in a spiral of uttering out-of-context remarks, thereby making the conversation unintelligible. I explained this to Dick and he immediately understood.

The new laptop became a composition device and a reading machine for student papers. Speaking was a lower priority because of the reasons I have described above and because scanning requires full concentration on the monitor, excluding the possibility of eye contact.

Dick mailed out a new version of Words+. It was for Windows, and had a TV control that was compatible with Windows. We never successfully installed the new Words+. We had lost our department computer specialist to downsizing. When we sent the laptop to the College of Social Sciences computer shop, they installed Windows 95, making Words+ inoperable. We are waiting for Dick to make one of his visits. He knows computers inside out and knows what Words+ is supposed to do. He also knows the details of my situation and what I am trying to accomplish with the laptop. This situational expertise is very rare.

8 Can He Think?

When I was hospitalized with serious pneumonia in 1991 and was on a huge blue respirator, the nurses would come into my room in the intensive care unit and ask my wife or my personal care attendant, "What did he do before?" There was the assumption I was no longer employed or had retired.

Robillard's Believe It or Not

This reaction was so common in the hospital that I began to think there is some bodily state that connotes being able to work. As I lay in the inflatable bed, with severe muscular dystrophy, unable to speak, and not being able to control my oral fluids, the mere perception of my body did not lead to the deduction that I was fully employed. The perception of my wasted body was so strong that even when Divina or my attendant would say, "Believe it or not, he is still working," the questioner would immediately turn the answer into a past tense. She or he would say, "I understand he was a professor before this hospitalization, but what does he do now?"

I am guilty of the same categorizations of the body. For example, when I had trouble with my portable suction machine, I began to question the mental competence of our medical supply representative because his obese body made me think he was a beer alcoholic. I have absolutely no information about the man's drinking behavior, but his huge belly let me categorize him as a drunkard who did not have the self-discipline and motivation to repair our suction machine. In fact, his obesity came with a priori categorizations of dissolute character. Bodies are inscribed with social categories—witness what we make of people who have blotchy, large noses with enlarged pores. What attributions do we routinely make about extremely thin young women? We carry around highly detailed categorizations about other persons according to body type and clothing.

The incident in the hospital about my employment is similar to one I encountered after I returned to work. I was up for reappointment, and I heard from a reliable source that the head of my department's promotion and tenure committee had said, "I know he is working, but what I want to know is can he think?" The chairman had seen me about four times, just after I got out of the hospital, when I was feeling especially weak and had the look of death about me. Three months in the ICU had wrung me out.

My pale look and extreme weight loss, coupled with muscle weakness, led him and others to question if I could work. The plain fact is that I did not have the look of one who could work. Although I had been paralyzed before the emergency hospitalization and had worked successfully, I felt the return to the university was a time in which I had to prove myself. I even felt that the past years of successful teaching and publishing were of little relevance to my colleagues and that this was a time to settle accounts of years' standing.

Even though I had been working successfully since the onset of my disease, the hospitalization for pneumonia made me feel like I had to start all over again. Some close colleagues suggested, while visiting me in the hospital, that I retire. The medical outlook among the hospital staff was bleak and it affected my colleagues. Staff members were not reticent about communicating my murky future, which could be picked up from their chronic use of the past tense when discussing me. This negative outlook was punctuated by my wife's having a beeper, when I was first hospitalized, so she could be summoned as I slid into death. No one expected me to recover.

One colleague, with my best interests at heart, came to the hospital and started to figure out my retirement income. He carefully calculated my social security and state retirement but quickly came to two conclusions. The first was that my retirement income would not be enough to cover minimal costs. The second was that I did not want to leave university life, and we should wait until I proved myself incapable of sustaining that life before we collectively decided I should retire.

The Lip-Reading System

Shortly after I returned from my Fulbright Professorship in the Philippines, I started to experience difficulty speaking. At first, I could manage these problems by over-articulating. But my upper palate was giving out and by 1987 I had lost the ability to speak clearly.

The most important thing for a professor is communicating. I was in deep trouble. I could not lecture. My speech had become unintelligible to most persons. Only those who were around me every day could understand me. I began to experience a loss of intelligibility to even close associates and family.

We figured out a lip-reading system. It was ad hoc, made up at home and in the office; there was no plan that we adopted. The main participants were my wife and my student research assistants. Divina was the principal creator of the system we developed.

When I began to lose my articulatory abilities, my wife and I continued to communicate by my mouthing familiar words. But Divina knew me very well, and she used this knowledge to decode what I was trying to say. Over six months we figured out a spelling system in which I would lip-sign or head-point specific letters. The development of a lip-signing system corresponded to my gradual loss of facial musculature control and of the ability to mouth recognizable words. My mother-in-law and my oldest daughter quickly learned the system my wife and I had organized.

For me to communicate with others, Divina borrowed an alphabet board from the Rehabilitation Hospital of the Pacific. We figured out a way of going down the rows of letters in which I would indicate the row the letter was on by raising my eyebrows. Once the row was selected, I would wait for the person to say the letter or point to it; then I would indicate which letter by again raising my eyebrows.

One difficulty quickly emerged with both the lip-reading system and the alphabet board. Many persons cannot spell, or at least cannot recognize spelled words. This problem was more evident with the alphabet board, though it also occurred with the lip-reading system. When I spell out a word like T H E, people will often not recognize it, even though it is a common word. Some will write the word down on a piece of paper, stare at it, and repeat the letters frequently; still, they cannot recognize T H E. When they finally get the word, they are startled at their inability to understand what they themselves had spelled out. I quickly came to learn that spelled-out communication is not the equivalent of spoken words.

Once my research assistants got involved in the lip-reading system, many improvements were introduced. These fine-tuned the indications of each letter and of some words. The letter C was a constant problem, and the solution, suggested by a student, was to look up and to the left to indicate it. Other problem letters were J, K, L, and Q, which occur on the right side of the alphabet chart or board. When I had trouble indicating these letters I would look at the board and lean to the right. Usually when I looked at the board, it meant I wanted the student assistant to look at the board and go through the rows and letters. But J, K, L, and Q were such frequent problems, accompanied by my leaning to the right, that this way of signing them was conventionalized. I would lean rightward and wait for the student to say the proper letter; raising my eyebrows showed that the one chosen was correct.

Likewise, when I lean to the left, I am trying to sign either G or X. I differentiate X from G by a swinging of my head from an upright position to one near my left shoulder. This movement approximates one of the strokes of the letter X. I indicate Z by looking up and shaking my head, approximating the directions of the letter.

I sign A by opening my mouth. B is signed by pressing my lips together, as is P. Signing D involves pressing my tongue to the top of my mouth. E is signed by opening my mouth with a raising or a crinkling of my nose. For F, I bring my upper teeth over my lower lip in repeated motion. Signing I involves opening my mouth, in a fashion similar to A. M is a pressing of the lips, often mistaken for B or P. There is no pressure exerted by my lips for M, however. I open my mouth in the shape of an O for that letter. R is an opening of my mouth while making the gesture of saying the letter, raising my palate. For S, as for H, I click my teeth. T involves putting my tongue in the front upper portion of my mouth and is often mistaken for D. I make the mouth movement of saying U for that letter. Bringing my upper teeth over my lower lip indicates V. The lipreader can distinguish V from F only from the context of the preceding letters and the context of what I am writing about. W involves waving my tongue in the middle of my mouth. For Y, I move my lips as I would say the letter.

The lip-signing system is a series of conventions of lip movements, head movements, and leaning. As I have noted, it was first developed by my wife and has evolved during ten years of interacting with my student assistants. The system is fluid, constantly in the process of refinement.

College and University Support

When I first started suffering symptoms of motor neuron disease, I had a series of National Institute of Mental Health grants for training mental health workers in Micronesia. I also had mental health research grants for Micronesia and a series of local health services research contracts. I was well financed and had as many as six students working for me.

As my disease advanced, I was not able to travel to Micronesia and to Washington. As I quickly became paralyzed, I found myself unable to get around the island of Oahu. Doing research by interviewing people, visiting clinics, and going through documents became problematic. The grants dried up. I did get some local health contract work, but the big grants simply expired.

I was in trouble. I could not teach or do research without lip-reading students. I was saved from oblivion by my colleagues in the College of Social Sciences. I had known the dean of the college for many years. This man, Deane Neubauer, a political scientist, had been particularly attentive at the beginning of my disease and had offered to co-teach with me. He resigned his deanship after a change of university administrations. Fortunately, he was followed in office by a psychologist, Dick Dubanoski, whom I had met in the Marshall Islands. Deane and Dick were extremely supportive and made sure I had the funding for lip-reading student assistants.

I feel the College of Social Sciences, through the influence of the two deans, has been the locus of my support. In addition to the student funding, I received a new computer, an extra-large monitor, and software designed for disabled people. I was also given a certificate by the college for service. All the financial support and the generous encouragement were offered in the spirit of keeping me working and even increasing my productivity beyond what I had achieved before my illness.

I think having the complete support of the two deans affected the sentiment toward me in my own department, sociology, and in other departments. Of course, I had my proponents in sociology. These sponsors, Kiyoshi Ikeda and Eldon Wegner, were the same friends who had supported me from the beginning of my association with the department.

I have co-taught with Deane Neubauer for nine years. He recruited Allan Howard, an anthropologist, to be involved with my seminar on social change in the Pacific Islands. I invited Jack Bilmes to co-teach with me in my ethnomethodology seminars. At first, Deane sat in on the course with Jack, modeling how to teach with a person who cannot vocalize. I have had co-teachers from anthropology, sociology, economics, American studies, ethnic studies, urban planning, communication, and linguistics.

Student Assistants

I had teaching assistants before my illness. But although I was close to some of them, I did not have the kind of relationship I have with most of my research assistants now. My association with the first lip-reading assistant came about by happenstance. I was in Manila as a Fulbright Professor and I had hired my first doctoral candidate, Marilyn Landis, to administer my two National Institute of Mental Health grants. She hired a student to help her, Jan Shishido. Jan worked for me for three years. She was with me as I lost my voice and was instrumental, along with Kathy Miller, in figuring out the lip-signing system.

Jan hired Kathy Miller, a daughter of a minister on Maui. We had to put together a book of papers that had been presented at a conference on Pacific Island mental health. Kathy, an English major, would stay for four years.

After Jan and Kathy moved on, we had to hire more research assistants and come up with a way to train them to lip-read. As usual, our method of selecting the students and training them was ad hoc. The next person we hired was Agatha Yap from Singapore, first of many native Chinese speakers. We tried to come up with a method of selecting students who would be good workers. We wanted people who were patient, not easily frustrated when they did not get the right letter when I signed, and who were trustworthy, responsible, and possessed of initiative. We wanted people who had computer skills or who could learn them fast. We looked for people who would stay after we had trained them. After some ugly fights between student staff, interpersonal skills became important, too. In short, we wanted what every employer wants.

As hard as we tried to come up with a systematic method of interviewing and selecting assistants, we found that hiring on the spur of the moment was no less effective than using a long and involved method of interviewing and debating the merits of each candidate. Most of those we have employed have worked out very well. About 25 percent did not. Some had bitter arguments with other students. There was a sudden resignation because of ongoing pressure from another assistant. One woman found it important to let it be known that she was from a rich landlord family and that the others were not of the same social origin. A few students did not show up for work, and one disappeared from the campus.

I rarely had to ask assistants to resign. I preferred to let them come to their own conclusion that things were not working out. Sometimes I would prompt a discussion of how an underperforming student thought she or he was doing. This talk would often lead to a decision to leave. I cannot remember a hostile resignation.

My research assistants often became my close friends. One of my enjoyments is supporting their career development and keeping in contact long after they have graduated. Because we would often gossip and because of the nature of their taking care of me (suctioning my mouth, transferring me from wheelchair to office chair, and wiping my nose, for example) close personal bonds developed. Divina and I would show our appreciation for the work the students did for me by taking them out to restaurants and having picnics.

Research

The base of my career at the University of Hawaii was training and research on mental health in Micronesia, focusing on the two-thousand-long string of islands called the Carolines. When my health started to fail, flying the long hours west from Hawaii and walking around coral roads in tremendous heat and humidity became very stressful. I went to Palau in 1986 and suffered a series of falls because of my dropped feet. (I could not pick up the front of my feet and would stumble over them.) My brothers-in-law had to walk alongside me, ever vigilant to catch me if I started to fall.

Maintaining my Micronesian career was bodily dependent. I had to fly frequently, passing through five time zones. More important, I had to have the physical mobility to get in small cars and the beds of pickup trucks, the ability to walk down long jungle paths, and the capacity to listen to subjects while squatting or sitting on the ground. I often used small outboard motorboats to visit lagoon islands. When I became paralyzed, I could not sustain my twice yearly visits to the Federated States of Micronesia and the Republic of Palau.

I had a strong attachment to Micronesia. It was where I had met my wife, and I had many close friends there. I had worked in the Federated States of Micronesia and the Republic of Palau for four years. An example of my personal identification with the region came during my last trip to Palau. My brothers-in-law had come from Manila for a visit with us and had their passports taken by customs at the airport. The next day I went to retrieve the passports in the office of the court. While I was standing at the counter of the clerk of the court, waiting and repeatedly asking for the passports, a secretary asked a passing Palaun traditional chief, "Who is this guy and what does he know about Palau?" The chief replied, "He knows everything about Palau. Give him what he wants." The passports were immediately turned over, and I experienced the warmth of knowing that I had strong connections with people who mattered in Palau.

I could not easily break the personal and professional identification I had with the Carolines. The Pacific Islands remained the focus of my teaching and research throughout the late 1980s and up until 1991. I created a new graduate seminar, Social Change in the Pacific Islands. It seemed strange that the University of Hawaii had no course on this topic, and I started to write articles and edit books on aspects of it. At Easter 1991, as I was editing a major volume on social change in the Pacific, I came down with pneumonia and was rushed to the hospital in an ambulance.

The prolonged stay in the intensive care unit of Queen's Hospital provided the opportunity to change the direction of my research. The depersonalization associated with intensive care directed me to examine the methods routinely used by nurses, physicians, respiratory therapists, physical therapists, social workers, and bioengineers to render care. I went back to my days at UCLA and my original training there as an ethnomethodologist. My wife encouraged this return to my intellectual roots.

When I was a graduate student at UCLA, I studied under Harold Garfinkel, the founder of ethnomethodology. He was very much influenced by the French phenomenologist Maurice Merleau-Ponty. This philosopher had formulated a description of how ordinary tasks are bodily accomplishments. To illustrate such bodily achievements, Garfinkel had his students build inverting lenses. Mounted in welding masks, the lenses turned everything upside down and reversed right and left. Garfinkel had us try to write our names on a blackboard while looking at it. We found we could not. Our handwriting broke down at every turn. The inverting lenses did not permit a routine access to knowing where your hand was, nor did they allow the visual monitoring and direction of where your hand was moving. If we closed our eyes, we were able to write our names legibly. But if we used our sight, the handwriting became confused, often provoking a momentary paralysis of the hand and arm. The objective of the exercise was to demonstrate that such mundane tasks as writing were founded on the habit of "normal" eyesight.

Garfinkel also had us experience speaking by means of a machine that delayed hearing your own voice as you spoke. We saw that intelligible speaking is based on the almost instantaneous capacity to hear yourself. If the delay became too great, the ability to pronounce even familiar words quickly degenerated into something that produced only mush-mouth mumbles.

With Garfinkel's encouragement, some of us tried to engage in group acts while wearing the inverting lenses. We set up a game. Three of us had large plastic garbage cans. The object of the game was to put each can inside another can. We were assigned a number for each round of the game. Number one was to put his can in the middle of the small lawn. Number two was to place his can inside that can. Number three was to put his can inside the can placed by number two.

We filmed the game. It was a catastrophe. Even when we marked the spot, none of the rotating number ones could reach the middle of the Beverly Hills lawn and place his can. The succeeding number twos and threes stumbled and fell when they tried to reach the can placed by the number ones. After a couple of hours, having overcome a strong sense of nausea, we were able to develop a new sense of bodily spatiality, matching our visual field to our executive sense of motility. We were able to accomplish the ends of the game, though with much lurching and a couple of falls.

In addition to the experiments with the inverting lenses and the speech delay machine, a small number of us took up Garfinkel's invitation to go down to Rancho los Amigos, the regional treatment center for spinal cord injuries. To prepare us for what to observe, Garfinkel gave us a detailed and elaborate manual on devices that assist the disabled in the tasks of everyday living. When we got to Rancho los Amigos we focused on asking the rehab patients how spinal cord injury had changed their ability to do routine household tasks. We received detailed technical descriptions of the impediments to their following normal routines successfully and how they overcame their physical disabilities.

I had never done anything with Garfinkel's teaching about the body. In late 1985, when my muscles were starting to waste, or atrophy, I experienced difficulties walking about our house. There was some spatial disorientation as I passed the wall of the kitchen. I was often dizzy and even had a spectacular fall in the kitchen. I started to think of Merleau-Ponty's writing about embodied spatiality, especially the sections on the phantom limb. I began to interpret my altered perception of the walls in our house, which seemed to waver, as being related to my altered musculature. But these reflections were momentary.

It was not until after my hospitalization for pneumonia in 1991 and the publication of my edited book on social change in the Pacific Islands in 1992 that I turned to writing an ethnomethodology of living in a disabled, weak, and mostly paralyzed body. Even when I wrote the first paper, on problems in communication, I had a hard time getting to the bodily order of speech between someone like me, who uses lip signing, and my intended recipient. I had been asked to describe and discuss my experience in the intensive care unit. I started out using an analytical frame, popular at the time, formulated by Jean Baudrillard. It had something to do with the signs of machines, particularly machines in the intensive care unit, replacing a previous system of signs.

I found the postmodern theory of signs a free-floating language that could not be tied to what I had experienced in the intensive care unit. I had the strong sense that I, as a person who could not communicate in what was a commonsense notion of "real time," was concertedly isolated by my caretakers and by my interaction with them. I returned to ethnomethodology as a way of making sense of my experience and living with it. The expectation that I had something to offer by way of ethnomethodological analysis of my situation made living much easier. I can say I had an ethnomethodological resolution of living in my altered body.

When I returned to ethnomethodology, I realized that to preserve the vision of this kind of analysis I could not practice other kinds of social analysis. I began to reflect on the work I had done on social change in Micronesia and on how I had incrementally gotten away from ethnomethodology, all the while thinking I was doing a form of ethnomethodology that incorporated the analyses of other paradigms of analysis. This realization hit me when I started to work on the bodily asynchronies that produced anger between me and my interlocutors. The vision of ethnomethodology about concerted, bodily production of intelligible interaction is fragile and contradicted by common sense. Although Garfinkel never said one cannot do other forms of analysis, I felt it was loudly implied. I now agree, and even explicitly teach this position.

I got into examining not only my own disability and the bodily disabilities of others but also the bodily production of order among so-called normal people. My students and I started to inspect the bodily order of what Erving Goffman named "withs": two or more people who are perceived to be together. We videotaped couples at the beach and people walking down the main street of Waikiki. We also started to examine the social production of rounds in the main teaching hospital of the University of Hawaii Medical School. This last topic is the focus of my current research.

Teaching

I teach in much the same way as I do research. I sit at the monitor of my computer and lip-sign to a student assistant, who types what I sign, letter by letter. Or, I may view videotapes, many of which are made by students themselves, that record behavior such as crowds crossing the street in downtown Honolulu or people eating lunch together in a park, and then return to typing out what I see. The videotapes are part of the classroom discussion on analyzing normal behavior.

I have three forms of teaching. The first is direct class teaching. I usually lead graduate seminars. Since I lost my voice, I have co-taught these; I plan the course, selecting the topics considering the expectations of the students. The plan of the seminar includes what we will do for every meeting. I normally write out the lectures, especially if it is a new course. Sometimes, even if the course is an old one, I will write out a list of topics for the day. Often, the co-teachers know me and the course so well that little paperwork is needed. I read and comment on drafts of students papers and I grade the final versions.

I normally sit in my wheelchair in class. A student research assistant sits to my right and I lip-sign what I want to say to the class; the student types what I sign on a laptop computer. When I am finished speaking, my assistant will verbalize what I have said to the class.

My co-teacher carries on the "real time" discussion in the seminar, following my plan. Sometimes the discussion will take the form of a mini-lecture, with students interrupting and asking questions. I will often make comments during the lectures. I will ask questions of the students, too.

Some problems have occurred in the seminars. Frequently it takes me so much time to lip-sign what I want to say that the conversation has moved on, and when I am ready to speak the class and co-instructor have forgotten the appropriate context of my remarks. I have to keep my turns at talk relatively short, lest the class conversation move too far for the fit of what I want to say. However, my remarks are too short and seem cryptic. I have to expand the cryptic ones.

Sometimes I will work with a student assistant who has difficulties breaking into the ongoing class conversation to insert my remarks. This problem takes two forms. The first involves the student who is shy about interrupting and waits so long to insert my utterances that they become dated. The second arises when my student assistant is not sensitive to the rhythms of the ongoing conversation and interrupts at any time, disorganizing the flow of talk.

Another difficulty presented itself when the students in one seminar requested more direct interaction with me in the class. I was very lucky to be teaching with a conversation analyst, Jack Bilmes, and he tried to slow down the pace of the class conversation so that I had more time to participate. This proved awkward at first, but things soon smoothed out.

The second way of teaching is in my office. I hold tutorials there with graduate students. I learned this form of teaching from Harold Garfinkel. The students sit to my right, where I can see their faces. I type into the monitor with the help of a student assistant and we can read what I say on the large screen. I find this form of instruction most satisfying.

The third form of teaching is reading student papers and commenting on them by e-mail. This indirect form of interaction is the least satisfying. I do it a lot, however, because I am on sixteen student graduate committees. I ask students to come in for direct tutoring if I am having trouble with their work.

Certain Gifts

When I could no longer walk, speak, feed myself, reach for and manipulate things, type on the computer, or even sign my name, these and the other features of paralysis made it look to many, including myself, that my working days as a professor of sociology were over. What actually happened was that I became a far more productive scholar and a better teacher than I was before my illness. This continues to surprise me.

Many factors, among them luck, have allowed me to keep working and become more productive than ever. I can mention only a few of these reasons. One, which I have alluded to above and will focus on in Chapter 9, is the quality of my training in the graduate program at UCLA. The instruction on bodily achievement let me capture and come to grips with my disability.

A second factor is that my wife is a Hawaii-licensed registered nurse. She resigned from her faculty position in the Department of Nursing at Kapiolani Community College, a unit of the University of Hawaii, to take care of me after my hospitalization in 1991. She attends to my immediate and daily medical needs, like suctioning my lungs, and drives me to and from work. She occupies the office next to mine, where she works on her own projects but is always available. She is instrumental in teaching the student office staff about how to get me out of the car and make other transfers.

My good fortune in recruiting and retaining student research assistants is also vitally important. This student staff has become the envy of my colleagues. They often ask how I consistently find such excellent research assistants. Except for the few problems mentioned above, I have been unusually lucky in finding people who are bright, patient, and personally secure and who have wonderful senses of humor. I interview the applicants myself, and I usually know who I want to hire after the first five minutes. I have to check out the students I want to hire with the other student research assistants, however, because I have been wrong in the past and hired some people who could not get along with the existing staff.

These assistants are my legs, arms, and whole bodies. They are also my trusted colleagues. I use them, for example, to enter my lip-signed letters into the computer. But they also go to the library, pick up the mail, get video equipment, tape scenes about town, turn pages and arrange documents, sign my name to forms, go with me to committee meetings and classes to translate, speak for me on the phone, read my papers before professional meetings, keep and maintain files, translate for me when I have visitors, get me out of the car and into and out of my office chair, translate for me when I am counseling students, suction my mouth, remind me of things to do, and carry out personal tasks. Beyond all this, they are also people I confide in and who will tell me how to do things better. These assistants are more than employees. There is also a constant dialogue going between the students and myself about their lives and my life (even if much of the talk is rank gossip).

Another factor that has allowed me to carry on is the support I have from my colleagues, both in my own department and throughout the College of Social Sciences. The support extends to my old associates in the Department of Pediatrics at Michigan State University, where I was a medical sociologist, to graduate school classmates, and to still other associates across the United States and the world. But I want to focus here on my colleagues at the University of Hawaii.

I have the impression that the support of my colleagues and my student research assistants at the university is unusual. I also think it stems from the aloha spirit of the culture of Hawaii, an ethic of personal caring. The spirit of aloha is a Native Hawaiian cultural trait, but it has infected all of the islands' immigrant groups. You can see it on the highway, in how men and women let you merge with traffic and easily defer to other drivers at crossroads, usually giving and receiving a wave. Those who do not comply with local driving courtesies are labeled as mainlanders or "not from here." I have witnessed the spirit of aloha many times when I need help getting out of the car or when I occasionally fall. Once, when my father-in-law flipped my wheelchair on top of me, two Hawaiian men came running from about three hundred yards away to pick me up and put me back in the seat.

This ethic of personal caring is palpable and stands as a measure of conduct. It is hardly talked about, except in the television advertising campaigns of the tourist authority—a futile effort to get locals to treat commercial visitors better. The attempt to mass produce aloha for the financial ends of tourism is usually resisted. But the spirit is taught and reproduced by example, as in driving, doing good deeds, and in the more general habit of caring about and taking responsibility for the welfare of others. I think this is why close colleagues (as well as persons who only know me by sight) corporately decide every year to give me student assistant funding and to, in part, renew my untenured contract.

The last reason I have space to mention is that my paralysis has added a new dimension to my concentration on work. When I was an able-bodied sociologist, I used to spend the major portion of the working day chatting in others' offices and attending meetings. I was engaged, like other academics, in producing the structure of the day through talk. I did not produce the publications I wanted to simply because I used up the working time with talk.

After my illness had set in and I was no longer consumed by searching the medical literature for a cure, I started to take a new attitude toward my work as a sociologist. I read a lot more and began to think of arguments counter and similar to those in the material I was reading. My thinking about such arguments is much more detailed than before; it led to dreaming of topic sentences and subordinate sentences and even the spatial layout of the paragraphs and page. I found that I could do my best writing in my head. If I had not thought out an argument the night before, it was best to wait until I had mentally composed it. The stillness of a paralyzed body increased my powers of concentration. I started to publish more than before, and I organized my classes down to the last detail.

I have come to think of my paralysis as bearing certain gifts. It is certainly not the case that I would not want to be able-bodied again. But I have learned from this experience the power of focused and sustained concentration and the increased productivity that stems from it.

9 The Trip

When my son Thomas won the art contest sponsored by Northwest Airlines, part of the prize was a free round trip to Minneapolis, site of corporate headquarters. Initially, I planned to go along. However, the trip soon proved a monumental and risky undertaking for me. I changed my mind. I would not go. It was very important, however, that my wife and son go.

I had been out of Divina's sight only for short durations, usually a half day. Organizing twenty-four-hour care for me was the impending problem for the spring and early summer. My main challenge lay in communicating with my caregivers. I had experienced the horror of not being able to talk to the nurses in the hospital. I am convinced that satisfactory care, for both my nurses and me, is a concerted achievement, produced through communication. Not being able to talk, I have experienced difficulties in my care, ranging from the banalities of having something done to me without my permission or at the wrong time, to not being able to tell caretakers my clothes were not on correctly, to the annoyance of being left in bed three days without my glasses. There have also been more serious situations: I saw the nurses were giving me the wrong medication; a nurse put intravenous medication down my trache; and I saw a nurse stick herself with a needle and then use the same needle to inject medicine into my body. The incapacity to talk, not being able to regulate my environment verbally, not being able to give warnings, have all convinced me of the truth of Murphy's Law: if something can go wrong, it will.

Let me give an example of the importance of being able to talk to nurses, fitting the emergent particulars of a treatment to my satisfaction. There is a part of my daily treatment routine called chest percussion. After my breathing treatment I have to lie on my side while someone uses a vibrator to loosen the phlegm built up in my lungs. Lying on my side is no easy task. The bed has to be lowered to a flat position. This can cause problems. Saliva quickly accumulates in the back of my mouth, causing me to choke and go into coughing spasms. Then, when I actually turn on my side, there can be additional problems from the placement of my shoulder and the position of my head and arms. My shoulders are highly atrophied, leaving little muscle tissue to take the load of my upper body weight. My neck has to be flexed, lest the saliva collect in my throat. One arm is often caught under the side of my body. It has to be pulled free and the hand has to be positioned so there are no curled fingers. My top arm must be placed so that its weight is not borne by the bones of an atrophied hand.

Given so many variables to remember, even the most conscientious person will make errors in doing the chest physical therapy. Depending on how I am lying on the bed, any number of mistakes can happen in situating me on my side for chest percussion. My arms can be positioned under me, leading to pain. My shoulders can dig into the mattress, causing considerable discomfort. My head can be placed so saliva collects in the back of my mouth, causing me to choke and cough, sometimes uncontrollably. Often, either because of pain associated with poor positioning or because of phlegm getting in the back of my mouth, the coughing gets so violent that the chest percussion has to be brought to a quick halt. One time in the hospital, the coughing became so explosive that I dislodged my trache and a pulmonologist had to be called to put it back in place.

If I can communicate with the caregiver directly or through an interpreter, I can indicate adjustments that need to be made in body positioning. Usually, I can anticipate a coughing spasm and indicate what changes need to be made. This requires the ability to communicate, through lip reading, with the caregiver. If I cannot communicate, I try to indicate something is wrong, often by using what limited body movement I have. Shaking my body or making what my wife calls "wide eyes" frequently leads to frustration and anger on the part of the caregiver. She or he has no idea of what I am trying to indicate. I, too, become angry and frustrated that the caregiver cannot understand me and, most often, continues the chest percussion under awful circumstances of pain or uncontrollable coughing spasms. This frequently starts off caregiving relationships on shaky grounds, from which they cannot easily recover.

Another illustration of concertedly produced adequate care is transfers. At six feet, one inch, I am a relatively tall man. I used to weigh two hundred pounds (although I have lost about thirty pounds, mostly from muscle atrophy). Nevertheless, I am not an easy transfer, moving from my bed to the toilet, from the toilet to my wheelchair, from my wheelchair to the car, from the car to the wheelchair, from the wheelchair to my office chair, from the office chair to my wheelchair, and finally back to the car. Additionally, I must be moved from the wheelchair to my easy chair in the family room, where I read and watch television.

Many things can go wrong in transfers. My arms and hands can be caught between my knees, which are usually pressed against one another during transfers. When this happens, I cannot stand up. Another thing that often happens is that my feet are placed so I cannot support my body weight during transfers. On such occasions, I often careen out of control, landing hard and painfully in places not intended. This can be quite dangerous and has caused injuries.

These mistakes can easily be avoided if the transferring person asks me if my arms are ready and if my feet are in the right place. Answering these questions can be problematic, though. When I shake my head back and forth, indicating no, the transferring person will frequently not recognize the negative, going ahead with the transfer. This often results in injuries, which can then affect subsequent transfers.

Chest percussion and transfers are only two examples of how my care is successfully or unsuccessfully produced in communication between me and my caregivers. The communication allows the adjustments that make chest percussion and transfers successful. This is what I call the concerted production of adequate care. This acting in concert, or communicating, permeates every aspect of my care. This was my main concern as we prepared for the trip.

Students

Language and speaking is often forgetful about itself. Speaking focuses on what is conveyed. How speaking or talk regulates every aspect of life is usually hidden. My wife, as dear as she is, has never fully understood the importance of ongoing talk between the caregiver and the person being cared for in making the many little adjustments that naturally arise in caregiving situations.

I was full of dread about my care when Divina would be in Minnesota with Thomas. I had been cared for by people who could not understand me when I was released from the hospital in 1991. This was a horrifying experience, full of mistakes in my care, all of which could have been avoided by simple communication.

My student assistants have been involved in my care since I came home in 1991. They have suctioned my mouth and helped Divina transfer me out of the car and from wheelchair to office chair. Some students asked to be taught how to suction my lungs. For a variety of vague reasons the instruction did not happen. However, in 1997, a student asked Divina many times to be taught how to suction. Finally, she saw the freedom this would bring her and assented to teach SueLyn Tran. First, she asked me if I were comfortable with her teaching SueLyn. I said I was completely comfortable.

After SueLyn learned to suction, various other student assistants asked to be taught. Divina trained them all, and SueLyn followed up with encouragement and further demonstrations. In a short while, I had four assistants who could suction. This was a big change. Until then, this had been exclusively my wife's job. She had been tied down by being near me in the office, since if I needed suctioning she would have to be there. With the students now able to do the job, she would frequently ask, "When is SueLyn working?" I would ask why. Divina's answer would be, "I feel I can leave you alone with SueLyn." She felt very comfortable with SueLyn doing the suctioning, as did I. This confidence soon extended to another assistant, Qian Miao.

Having two students who could suction proved to be an invaluable asset. Most professional nurses do not see patients with a tracheotomy. Although they may be taught how to suction in nursing school, for ten minutes, the absence of practice on suitable patients leaves them ill prepared for the real thing. Breathing is my biggest concern.

Now, with SueLyn and Qian, I had two suctioners who practiced every day. They became excellent suctioners. Moreover, I could communicate rapidly with them by lip reading. I could tell them what lung to suction, how much to suction, and when to stop.

I came up with the idea that students would be in the house twenty-four hours a day during the trip. This took care of two worries. The first was about communicating with the nurses we would hire. The second worry was about having good suctioners. By the time of the trip, all four of my research assistants had learned suctioning. We wrote a schedule, where students and professional nurses would work twelve-hour shifts.

Trip

Divina, Thomas, and Terry, my son from my first marriage, left Honolulu on a Thursday. Even though we had planned my care thoughtfully, I was still highly apprehensive. I felt a little like I was being abandoned. The feeling would change quickly.

I had decided that I would not go to work during the trip. Less than a week was involved, and I thought it would be too much trouble getting me from my house to work, twenty miles away. The feeling about the difficulty of going to work in my wife's absence would also change. In fact, I would experience a sense of exhilaration, a sort of emancipation, through organizing a group of students who could care for me, independently of my wife, and take me to and from school. But I would come to feel this way only months after the Minnesota trip.

Day one was passed watching television, mostly CNN, with some Chinese soap operas thrown in. Qian Miao, who worked the first day shift, translated the Chinese shows. However, as we all discovered, the soap operas of the world share the same plot and acting. The day would pass without incident.

The night was a hurdle. When I said let's go to bed, sometime during the David Letterman show, we transferred me to the wheelchair and then to the bed. Never mind that the transfers were shaky, needing three people to complete. The real problem was getting my night treatment done. This was the first time for the night nurse and two students. My wife had prepared a set of instructions in a red loose-leaf binder. This quickly came to be known as "the red book." Reading the instructions and carrying out each step of the evening routine of care took over three hours. It normally takes Divina forty-five minutes to an hour. I went to sleep at three in the morning.

The plan was to have the nurse sleep in my wife's bed, next to my hospital bed. The student would sleep in my son's room and would be awakened if I needed translation. The night nurse was an extraordinarily sweet man named Lloyd. He rode a real street hog, a big Harley-Davidson. Unfortunately, Lloyd's snoring was as loud as his motorcycle. I could not sleep. I tried beeping him out of it with my alarm, mounted on my pillow. I beeped ten times, but I could neither wake Lloyd nor stop his snoring. After twenty beeps, I woke him and told him I could not sleep because of his snoring. He told me his wife had been complaining of the same thing. He remarked that she was strongly urging surgery to resolve the problem. He suctioned me and went back to bed. Within ten minutes the Harley-Davidson snore had resumed. When I was finally able to rouse him I said, "I cannot sleep and I am very tired." Lloyd apologized effusively. "I will try not to snore," he said. We went back to sleep. Within five minutes the racket of the snoring had resumed. Again I woke up Lloyd. Again he said, "I am so sorry." Again we went back to sleep. But this time I could not sleep. It was already getting light. I got only one hour of sleep. I was exhausted.

At seven in the morning, we started the morning treatments. The breathing treatment was delayed because they could not figure out how to assemble the circuit on my vent in the proper sequence. The alarm kept going off on the ventilator. After half an hour, we began. The next step is chest percussion. This involves being laid down flat on the bed and then being turned on my side. This step had to be restarted about ten times that morning because of poor positioning. To make an involved story short, it took six hours to accomplish the morning treatment routine. It normally takes two. I got to my chair in the family room at one in the afternoon.

The second day was hard on everyone. Most of my caregivers were tired and irritable, and I was extremely out of sorts. During the afternoon, I began to think of checking myself into Queen's Hospital. I did not see how I could endure four more days of not sleeping and exhausting treatment routines. Another factor provoking anxiety was that I was not getting adequate deep suctioning. I could feel an incremental buildup of fluid in my lungs. At this time, only SueLyn could deep suction. My wife was telephoned in the early evening and my worries and thoughts of checking myself into the hospital were relayed to her. She told me it was my call.

During the early evening Anthony Bichel, a graduate student then finishing his dissertation, had a brilliant idea: "Why not ask SueLyn to sleep with you? She is the best suctioner and I assume she doesn't snore." He said, "I am going to ask SueLyn when she gets here." She gave her assent. I was so tired from the previous evening and day that I slept the whole night, waking SueLyn only once. I was very happy she was a silent sleeper. I was fully refreshed the next day and in good humor.

The remaining days were uneventful, except for a minor amount of tension between two students. Most of us could not comprehend this tension, but it also made most of us laugh. When my wife returned, she immediately suctioned me, saying, "No one suctions like me." Which is true.

Breast Biopsy

Little did I know that the organization of care for me during the trip would be a rehearsal for things to come. Divina had noticed a lump in her right breast. She had a core stereotactic and needle biopsy. The results were negative for cancer. Yet, the lump continued to grow. My wife sought a different surgeon. This surgeon, a woman, advised that the "developing" lump be removed.

Divina wanted to wait until after the trip to have the lump removed. She returned from Minneapolis in August and scheduled the lumpectomy for September. I went with her to meet the new surgeon and to learn about the procedures for the lumpectomy. We began our cancer education, all the while hoping the lump would be benign. The lumpectomy was on a Friday in late September. Qian did the day, as during the trip, and SueLyn did the night.

We had a new person helping us, Eric Ishiwata, a recently hired research assistant from San Jose, California. He would quickly become a pivotal person in my life and in the lives of everyone who was close to me. Eric is a graduate student in American studies.

The following Monday, the surgeon called my office and asked us to meet with her immediately. I was extremely nervous but kept telling my wife, "It can still be good news." However, the request that we come right away to her office had scary portents. When we arrived we were ushered into an examination room. We waited for the surgeon. When she came in she immediately said, "I don't have good news. The lump I removed was cancerous and the surrounding tissue was cancerous." We were desolated. Divina and I were both thinking, "We have enough coping to do with one illness. This is too much." As the surgeon went on, explaining the need for a modified radical mastectomy, we were too numb to follow her. It would take another visit to really learn and understand what the surgeon was proposing.

I was in shock for weeks. I tried to learn as much about breast cancer as possible. I went to Borders bookstore and had Eric buy *Dr. Susan Love's Breast Book.* I e-mailed friends all over the country. One of them, Karen Ito of UCLA, faxed me many clinical studies of breast cancer and its treatment. My son Terry, a student at UCLA, faxed me and told me of articles on treating breast cancer. He led me to interesting Web sites on breast cancer, as well. My sister, Robin, a breast cancer survivor, also alerted us to significant Web sites and books. Two old friends, Bill Weil and Rich Frankel, of the medical schools at Michigan State University and the University of Rochester, respectively, added useful information and encouragement.

By the time of the mastectomy, I was saturated with information about breast cancer and its treatment and outcomes. I spent hours on the World Wide Web. I had requested a second pathology report from UCLA on the materials from the lumpectomy. I got tired of waiting and asked Karen Ito to follow it up. She gave me the home fax number of the pathologist and I faxed him a letter of inquiry. He, in turn, faxed me a very interesting answer to my questions. This, too, was part of my education on breast cancer.

Surgery

We tried to get our insurance company to pay for twenty-four-hour nursing for two weeks. We were worried the firm would not go for it, having funded the nursing for the trip to Minnesota that summer. We visited our primary care physician, Steven Berman, and he argued persuasively that this was an emergency and it would cost the insurance company much more to put me in the hospital, which he would do if they did not fund home nursing. Berman submitted a request to the insurance company to pay for two weeks of twenty-four-hour nursing. The company responded that it would fund one week of twenty-four-hour care and one week of twelve-hour care.

We had to recruit nurses through the same home nursing agency we had used for years. We started off with our favorite nurse, Patrice Scott. She had taken care of me for five years, and I really liked her. However, we needed four nurses to cover the whole two weeks, with each one working a twelve-hour shift. We tried to recruit Lloyd, who had nursed me during the trip. Unfortunately, he had suffered a significant brain injury in a motorcycle accident and was not immediately available. We recruited three additional nurses. One I knew, and two were military service nurses.

The next task was setting up the schedule of students; they would interpret for me and participate in my care. Eric Ishiwata, a rock climber with amazing upper body strength, had become the premier transfer agent. By now, he, Scott Okamoto, Ginette Alipio, and Qian Miao had developed into first-class suctioners. We were able to plan ten days of student coverage, leaving the rest to be arranged when we got going.

The mastectomy took place on November 7, a Friday. I stayed home with Qian and Patrice, the nurse. The day went smoothly. I waited to hear news of the surgery. SueLyn Tran had gone to the hospital, and she had seen Divina in the recovery room and then in her own room. My mother-in-law called and reported my wife' s condition and told me that SueLyn was there. Later, Divina herself called and told us how she felt. M.J. Amundson, a friend from the School of Nursing, stayed the night with my wife. The next day, Saturday, my wife called and told us she had asked the surgeon for another night in the hospital. This was a good idea. Caring for me took several people and plenty of energy, and Divina has always been distracted by how I am faring. It was better to leave her out of the scene at home. She could at least rest in the hospital.

Saturday morning I had a lot of trouble with a nurse. These were not my first difficulties with her. She was nervous and got rattled easily. When I communicated "no" to this nurse, she would go ahead and do the very thing I had just said no to. I could not communicate with or control this person. Having the students there to translate for me did not seem to help. For the first time, I fired a nurse. I had asked the agency not to send specific individuals back, but this was the first time I had confronted a particular nurse on the job. I told her, "Don't come back." She became unnerved and cried.

Firing the nurse upset a lot of people. However, I experienced taking control over the quality of those caring for me as a breakthrough. I had suffered through lots of poor-quality nurses. Some were chronically late, some left in mid-shift without telling anyone (even me) where they were going, some came to work drunk, and one sniffed cocaine while taking care of me. But the most irritating thing about nurses is that most of them considered my wife to be the person in charge, relegating me to the status of an infant. Even if Divina told them, "He is in charge and he is paying the bills for your time," the nurses would only take instructions from my wife. (There were, however, a few notable exceptions.) The nurse I fired was particularly controlling, and she would not respond to my requests. Taking the action I did represented finally assuming executive power over the people who took care of me.

But firing the nurse required that I replace her. I immediately thought of Lloyd. I called him, and to my surprise discovered that he was ready to work. Lloyd is the kind of nurse I like. He does nothing to me without asking permission or finding out if I am ready. He is easygoing and does not get rattled. When he showed up for work, most of the students and other nurses were shocked to see he had lost fifty pounds. He was not noticeably fat when he stayed with me during the Minneapolis trip. But the motorcycle accident and the brain injury had left him with no appetite and no sense of taste.

The weekend went by without any problems. Divina came home Sunday afternoon. She appeared devoid of energy and had two surgical drains in her wound. These drains would have to be "milked," meaning the half-dried blood clots in the tubes would need to be manually moved down to the collection bags at the end of the tubes. Charon Pierson, a graduate student (and nurse) and SueLyn Tran would do this.

Monday presented a new challenge. I had stayed home during the trip and the lumpectomy. My reasoning was that going to work presented too many opportunities to get injured during transfers and to get into breathing problems due to inadequate suctioning. Yet, this was in the middle of the fall semester. I was teaching and I was late with the manuscript for this book. I was also worried about the impression an absence from work would make on my chairman, colleagues, and the director of my research institute. I am afflicted with a strong work ethic, amplified, I think, by my disability.

This is where Eric Ishiwata became pivotal. First, he is a fellow you think you have known forever after a couple of months. Second, Eric is an extremely positive person, always encouraging me that we could and should go to work. Third, he is strong and capable. Although I had feared difficulties in going to work without my wife, I felt comfortable that Eric would successfully manage the task. He did all the driving and transfers for three weeks.

During the first week, we had nurses around the clock. The day nurse would go with me to the university. I preferred that the students do the suctioning. I only had to look at SueLyn and Qian in a particular way, and they knew if I needed mouth or trache suctioning. They were so accustomed to me and my routine that they had a tremendous sense of anticipation. Later, Divina would tell the students, particularly Qian and SueLyn, to do the suctioning because they had a cleaner technique.

The first week went fine. Either Qian or SueLyn would spend the night, sleeping in the next bed and waking whenever I beeped them to suction me. They would assist the nurses in my evening and morning treatments. Eric would get me up and out of bed, dressed, and into and out of the car.

The second week, when we had only twelve hours of nursing, was a challenge. My wife suggested and arranged that the nurses split their shifts into eight-hour day and four-hour night segments. This way they would be able, with the assistance of SueLyn, Qian, and Eric, to perform the morning and night treatments. During this time, Divina was able to get a full night's sleep in our son's room. She had taken care of me continuously since my discharge from the hospital in 1991. I saw this opportunity, in part, not only as an occasion for her to recover but to get a well-deserved rest from caring for me.

I relied on the students more than ever during the second week. Except for Qian getting an eye infection, the days went by easily. SueLyn and Eric had to fill in for her for a couple of days. When Qian stopped taking the Western and Chinese eye medicine, however, her eye immediately cleared up and she returned to both office and home work.

Feeling of Emancipation

My wife has taken excellent care of me. She is the single reason I am still alive, defying all prognostications. Such long-term care cannot be without complaint, however. I know most caregivers complain. I complained when I was taking care of my dying father in Florida. I like to remember my complaints as muted. My wife has complained, on bad days, that my illness has drained her, that constant pressure of taking care of me has ruined her life and the life of our son. She has asked me to be creative in thinking of ways, within our limited means, to free her from the constraints of having to be around me constantly.

I tried to think of ways to free my wife. We hired nurses to come every Saturday, and often at work. This was only a limited freeing, though, due to the costs of insurance coverage. The real breakthrough came independently of my efforts or my wife's deliberations. SueLyn Tran asked to be taught how to suction, saying there was no reason to bother Divina with the job. This freed and continues to free my wife for whole afternoons. Qian Miao quickly followed in learning to suction. SueLyn also took over tube-feeding and cleaning my trache area and changing the trache dressing. She then taught Qian how to do this, which further increased Divina's independence.

The real feeling of emancipation would come during the period of my wife's surgery. I think it was sometime during the second week that I realized that SueLyn, Qian, and Eric composed a unit of care that permitted me some independence. I especially remember the exhilaration of riding around Honolulu at night after work. I was with the three students. I had not cruised in a car for years, and I felt like I had shed decades. I started coming home later than usual. I had achieved what a close friend, Deane Neubauer, had recommended: "Give Divina an envelope of time to recover, where she does not have to worry about you."

I have always thought I was close to my research assistants. However, I am so tightly bound with the present group that many persons have described us as a family. I feel closer to Qian, SueLyn, and Eric than to my blood relatives. It must be because of the opportunities we had to engage in endless talk during the trip, biopsy, and three weeks of surgery recovery. I admire each of them because they are extraordinarily bright. It may also be that the personal relationship with my research assistants began with Qian, long before the trip. Qian is an extremely intelligent woman from Beijing, who has long made observations about my behavior and the behavior of others. Most of her observations are true.

I found that achieving the envelope where my wife could rest was not as welcome as I had imagined. Although Divina very much appreciated the help she and I were receiving from the students, she was somewhat envious and a little resentful of my emotional bond with them. I found it wise for a while to not talk about the student research assistants in her presence. Later, my wife would joke about my relations with the students, relieving a lot of unstated tension.

Separating Divina from caregiving was far more complicated than I had imagined. In retrospect, I am gratified by the commitment she has continued to show to my care, even while suffering the discomforts of surgery, the emotional trauma of a mastectomy, and the debilitating effects of chemotherapy.

The Arrival of Siblings

Divina's two brothers and sister came to our house shortly after the mastectomy. Divina's parents had petitioned the U.S. Immigration and Naturalization Service for their daughter and two sons when they arrived in Hawaii in 1986. The parents have lived with us since then.

I think my wife and I idealized the physical help the siblings would give us. I told the students that Divina's sister and two brothers would take over the jobs they were doing. I now realize this was an unrealistic expectation. The siblings have been a tremendous help, mainly in transfers. They have been of even more assistance in providing my wife emotional support. Merely having them in the house brings conclusion to the family chain migration from the Philippines to the United States.

While my wife's siblings are a source of emotional support, I find the intergenerational reproduction of behaviors in the family interesting. I have always been amazed at the sleeping patterns of my father-in-law. He can sleep twenty hours a day; I used to call him Rip Van Winkle. Now, I am able to observe that his daughter and two sons sleep at least ten hours a night and like to take an afternoon nap of two hours. Everyone in my house, except me, my son Thomas, and my wife is asleep by eight in the evening. I now call my father-in-law the "sleep leader."

The approach to sleep is a measure of the broad difference in values between myself and my wife's family. Their approach conflicts with my Protestant upbringing. When I ask my brothers-in-law why they sleep so much, they answer, "There is nothing to do." For me, the reason there is nothing to do is that you are sleeping and not using your mind to come up with new projects. There is, of course, another way of looking at this: perhaps I am condemned by the activism of the Protestant Ethic.

This commitment to prodigious sleeping is only an indirect reason the siblings have been of limited help. I cannot communicate with them. We have tried to teach them lip reading but they rarely interact with me. When they are awake, they sit in one room and I sit alone in the family room. We do not chat or have time to practice lip reading. When I try to initiate communication with them, they give short answers and scoot out of the room. When I complain to Divina that I cannot talk to them, practice lip reading, get to know them, she tells me I have an intimidating personality and they are scared to interact with me. I think it is a lot more than that.

I came to the conclusion that we had to rely on the students to get us through the chemotherapy. I can communicate with them, I trust them, and I like them. We had to call Qian in the middle of the night the first night of chemotherapy. She came and took care of me, letting Divina sleep without interruption. The second chemotherapy session, one week later, produced less of a shock. We asked SueLyn to come. We continued to rotate the two women to take care of me on chemotherapy days.

Chemotherapy ended in late May. The last two weeks of chemotherapy were the most difficult. Divina vomited continuously. She lost weight. She thought she was going to die. We called SueLyn often, asking her to come over in the middle of the night or in the early morning.

It took a month for Divina to recover from the chemotherapy. She was tired. But she quickly recovered her strength and started to transfer me by herself.

A month after chemotherapy, her oncologist suggested radiation treatment. This started in late August and continued to early October. At first, radiation seemed easy. But in the last two weeks, Divina's white blood cell count went down and she caught a cold. For about two weeks she suffered vertigo. She felt the room spin and she had to hold onto the walls. She could not drive. Again, the student assistants drove me to school and took care of me.

In other chapters I have written about the cultural typifications of disabled people, especially those who are paralyzed. I have described how these underlying typifications limit and distort what the paralyzed person can do. I have noted the effects on conversation, the exclusion from social participation and the resulting isolation, the slips of the tongue that hurt so much, the rush to help with high technology that only increases isolation, and the typifications that make continued employment as a professor a contingent phenomenon. If the assaults do not come from the actual disease, they come from the cultural typifications of individuals afflicted by it. The cultural notions of competence are not forgiving.

How do I cope with this seeming onslaught? Paralysis has taught me patience. Not being able to speak has been very frustrating. But it has also enabled me to watch the formulation of social structure through conversation, as people talk. Being patient and seeing what most people take for granted (and therefore do not see) has not resolved my emotions, however. I am still subject to needs and wants, which I share with most people. I am subject to moods, good and bad. I am in the same social flux as anyone. When I take a reflective step back, usually after a period of stress, I remember that this life cannot be figured out and will always have the moving mystery of the Tao. I can only deal with small features, and then only with those that I have skills for. And even successful dealing will not hide the fact that life is a mystery, like a journey, and that there are no ultimate reasons.

References

Atkinson, Maxwell J., and John Heritage, eds. 1984. *Structure of Social Action: Studies in Conversation Analysis.* Cambridge: Cambridge University Press.

Baudrillard, Jean. 1983. *In the Shadow of the Silent Majorities; or, The End of the Social and Other Essay.* Translated by Paul Foss, John Johnston, and Paul PaHon. New York: Semiotext(e).

———. 1993. *The Transparency of Evil: Essays on Extreme Phenomena.* Translated by James Benedict. London: Verso.

Bellman, Beryl. 1975. *Village of Curers and Assassins: On the Production of Fala Kpelle Cosmological Categories.* The Hague: Mouton.

Bertocci, Peter A. 1988. *The Person and Primary Emotion.* New York: Springer Verlag.

Boden, Deirdre, and Don Zimmerman, eds. 1991. *Talk and Social Structure: Studies in Ethnomethodology and Conversation Analysis.* Oxford: Polity Press.

Burke, Mary, and Susan Sherman, eds. 1993. *Gerontological Nursing: Issues and Opportunities for the Twenty-First Century.* New York: National League for Nursing Press.

Cicourel, Aaron V. 1964. *Method and Measurement in Sociology.* New York: Free Press.

Condon, William S. 1974. "Neonate Movement Is Synchronized with Adult Speech: Interactional Participation and Language Acquisition." *Science* 183:99–101.

———. 1979. "Neonatal Entertainment and Enculturation." In *Before Speech: The Beginning of Interpersonal Communication,* edited by Margaret Bullowa. Cambridge: Cambridge University Press.

Condon, William S., and Louis W. Sander. 1974. "Neonate Movement Is Synchronized with Adult Speech: Interactional Participation and Language Acquisition." *Science* 183:99–101.

Coulter, Jeff. 1975. "Perceptual Accounts and Interpretive Asymmetries." *Sociology* 9, no. 3:385–96.

Davis, Martha, ed. 1982. *Interaction Rhythms: Periodicity in Communicative Behavior.* New York: Human Sciences Press.

Epstein, Arnold L. 1992. *In the Midst of Life: Affect and Ideation in the World of the Tolai.* Berkeley and Los Angeles: University of California Press.

Fine, Michelle. 1992. *Disruptive Voices: The Possibilities of Feminist Research.* Ann Arbor: University of Michigan Press.

Frankel, Richard M. 1983. "The Laying of Hands: Aspects of the Organization of Gaze, Touch, and Talk in a Medical Encounter." In *The Social Organization of Doctor-Patient Communication,*19–54. Washington: Harcourt Brace Jovanovich.

Franks, David D., and E. Doyle McCarthy. 1989. *The Sociology of Emotions.* Greenwich, Conn.: JAI Press.

Garfinkel, Harold. 1967. *Studies in Ethnomethodology.* Cambridge: Polity Press.

———. 1986. *Ethnomethodological Studies of Work.* London: Routledge.

———. 1996. "Ethnomethodology's Program." *Social Psychology Quarterly* 59, no. 1:5–21.

Garfinkel, Harold, Michael Lynch, and Eric Livingston. 1981. "The Work of a Discovering Science Construed from Materials from the Optically Discovered Pulsar." *Philosophy of the Social Sciences* 11: 131–58.

Garfinkel, Harold, and D. Lawrence Wieder. 1992. "Two Incommensurable, Asymmetrically Alternate Technologies of Social Analysis." In *Text in Context,* edited by Graham Watson and Robert M. Seiler, 175–206. London: Sage.

Gartner, Alan, and Tom Joe, eds. 1987. *Images of the Disabled, Disabling Images.* New York: Praeger.

Gibson, William. 1984. *Neuromancer.* New York: Ace Books.

Girton, George D. 1986. "Kung Fu: Toward a Proxiological Hermeneutic of the Martial Arts." In *Ethnomethodological Studies of Work,* edited by Harold Garfinkel, 60–91. London: Routledge and Kegan Paul.

Glick, Robert A., and Steven P. Roose. 1993. *Rage, Power, and Aggression.* New Haven, Conn: Yale University Press.

Goffman, Erving. 1963. *Stigma: Notes on the Management of Spoiled Identity.* New York: Simon and Schuster.

Goodwin, Charles. 1981. *Conversational Organization: Interaction between Speakers and Hearers.* New York: Academic Press.

———. "Professional Vision." *American Anthropologist* 96, no. 3:606–33.

Hauck, Paul A. 1974. *Overcoming Frustration and Anger.* Philadelphia: Westminster Press.

Heidegger, Martin. 1962. *Being and Time.* Translated by John Macquarrie and E.S. Robinson. London: SCM Press.

Husserl, Edmund. 1991. *Cartesian Meditations: An Introduction to Phenomenology.* Translated by Dorion Cairns. Dordrecht: Kluwer.

Jameson, Fredric. 1987. "The Politics of Theory: Ideological Positions in the Postmodernism Debate." In *Interpretive Social Science: A Second Look,* edited by Paul Rabinow and William N. Sullivan, 351–64. Berkeley and Los Angeles: University of California Press.

Kendon, Adam, ed. 1981. *Nonverbal Communication, Interaction, and Gesture.* The Hague: Mouton.

Kleinman, Sherryl, and Martha A. Copp. 1993. *Emotions and Fieldwork.* Newbury Park, Calif.: Sage.

Kübler-Ross, Elisabeth. 1981. *Living with Death and Dying.* New York: Macmillan.

Landy, Frank J. 1985. *Psychology of Work Behavior.* Homewood, Ill.: Dorsey Press.

Levy, Robert. 1973. *Tahitians: Mind and Experience in the Society Islands.* Chicago: University of Chicago Press.

Livingston, Eric. 1986. *The Ethnomethodological Foundations of Mathematics.* London: Routledge and Kegan Paul.

Lynch, Michael. 1985. *Art and Artifact in Laboratory Science.* London: Routledge and Kegan Paul.

———. 1993. *Scientific Practice and Ordinary Action: Ethnomethodology and Social Studies of Science.* Cambridge: Cambridge University Press.

Merleau-Ponty, Maurice. 1962. *Phenomenology of Perception.* Translated by Colin Smith. London: Routledge and Kegan Paul.

Murphy, Robert. 1987. *The Body Silent.* New York: Henry Holt.

Narens, Louis. 1985. *Abstract Measurement Theory.* Cambridge, Mass.: MIT Press.

Parsons, Talcott. 1978. *Action Theory and the Human Condition.* New York: Free Press.

Pollner, Melvin. 1987. *Mundane Reason: Reality in Everyday and Sociological Discourse.* Cambridge: Cambridge University Press.

Psathas, George, ed. 1990. *Interaction Competence.* Lanham, Md.: University Press of America.

Psathas, George. 1995. *Conversation Analysis: The Study of Talk-in-Interaction.* Thousand Oaks, Calif.: Sage.

Radley, Alan. 1995. "The Elusory Body and Social Constructionist Theory." *Body & Society* 1, no. 2:3–23.

Rexford, Eveoleen N., Louis W. Sander, and Theodore Shapiro, eds. 1976. *Infant Psychiatry: A New Synthesis* (New Haven: Yale University Press).

Rosengren, William R. 1980. *Sociology of Medicine: Diversity, Conflict, and Change.* New York: Harper and Row.

Sacks, Harvey. 1995. *Lectures on Conversation.* Cambridge, Mass.: Blackwell.

Schegloff, Emanuel A. 1991. "Reflections on Talk and Social Structure." In *Talk and Social Structure: Studies in Ethnomethodology and Conversation Analysis,* edited by Deirdre Boden and Don H. Zimmerman, 44–71. Cambridge: Polity Press.

Schutz, Alfred. 1967. *Collected Papers.* Vol. 1, *The Problem of Social Reality,* edited by Maurice Natanson. The Hague: Martinus Nijhoff.

Siegman, Aron W., and Timothy Smith, eds. 1994. *Anger, Hostility, and the Heart.* Hillsdale, N.J.: Lawrence Erlbaum Associates.

Smith, Dorothy. 1987. *The Everyday World as Problematic: A Feminist Sociology.* Boston: Northeastern University Press.

Stearns, Carol Z., and Peter N. Stearns. 1986. *Anger: The Struggle for Emotional Control in America's History.* Chicago: University of Chicago Press.

Toombs, S. Kay. 1992. *The Meaning of Illness: A Phenomenological Account of the Different Perspectives of Physician and Patient.* Dordrecht: Kluwer.

Treichler, Paula A., Richard M. Frankel, Cheris Kramarae, Kathleen Zoppi, and Howard B. Beckman. 1984. "Problems and Problems: Power Relationships in a Medical Encounter." In *Language and Power,* edited by Cheris Kramarae, Muriel Schulz, and William O'Barr, 62–88. Beverly Hills, Calif.: Sage.

Tucker, Kenneth H., Jr. 1993. "Aesthetics, Play, and Cultural Memory: Giddens and Habermas on the Postmodern Challenge." *Sociological Theory* 11, no. 2:194–211.

Woodward, Bob. 1994. *The Agenda: Inside the Clinton White House.* New York Simon and Schuster.

Zola, Irving. 1982. *Missing Pieces: A Chronicle of Living with a Disability.* Philadelphia: Temple University Press.

Index

DATE			